THE OLDEST WORD FOR DAWN

THE OLDEST WORD FOR DAWN

New and Selected Poems

BRAD LEITHAUSER

Alfred A. Knopf NEW YORK 2013

Library of Congress Cataloguing-in-Publication Data

Leithauser, Brad.
  [Poems. Selections]
  The oldest word for dawn : new and selected poems / by Brad Leithauser.—First edition.
    pages cm
  ISBN 978-0-307-95965-2
  I. Title.
  PS3562.E4623043 2013   811'.54—dc23   2012042633

Jacket image: Measured Morning, *1995 by Mark Leithauser (detail).*
Jacket design by Linda Huang

Manufactured in the United States of America
First Edition

FOR
MY TWO
TRUE AMPLITUDES—

Emily Salter Leithauser
and
Hilary Garner Leithauser

by dawn-light and gone-light

EVENING: A WATERCOLOR

Only a few of us rode
   in the gathering dark.
On the glistening pavement,
   lights mirrored themselves in a chain—
Linked-gold where the bus swung wide
   to circle the park,
Blue-green where the factory windows
   started again.

Nobody spoke, but the way
   did not seem at all long.
The sibilant tires reassured us
   in thrumming refrain,
And the bus driver whistled
   the cool little flakes of a song
That hovered a moment like snow
   and were lost in the rain.

GLADYS GARNER LEITHAUSER

1925–2010

CONTENTS

AUTHOR'S NOTE

A poet, too, must have his fictions, and the notion of an ideal reader has long been of considerable help to me. In my case, this is someone who shares my love of animals, including weird prosodic animals; who senses poetry in numbers; who sees no reason why even an emotionally complicated human story might not naturally unfold in verse. This ideal reader has provided over the years not merely confirmation but inspiration.

What I think of as my math poem, "An All but Empty Set," is dedicated to my personal Ramanujan, Kannan Jagannathan. "Little Dig" is for Lawrence Douglas and Nancy Pick; "The Birth of Injustice" for Ann Close; "Altamira" for John Varriano and Wendy Watson; "The Horse in the Gallery" for Jean McGarry; "The Other Side" for John Hennessy and Sabina Murray; "Moon Over" for Joan Abrahamson; "Sleeping through a Blizzard" for Marietta Pritchard; "Bad Breaks" for Greg Williamson; "Long Odds" for John McComb; "Earlier" for Jack Cameron; "Remote Midnights" and "Distant Dawns" for the Chapman family: John, Patty, Nicky and Paul; "Sleeping by the Shore" for Nancy Chapman.

And "Small Building" is for Sheila Patrice McCormick.

New Poems

I. INWARD ISLAND

OLD GLOBE

For her big birthday
we gave her (nothing less would do)
the world, which is to say

a globe copyrighted the very year
she was born—eighty years before.
She held it tenderly, and it was clear

both had come such a long way:
the lovely, dwindled, ever-eager-to-please
woman whose memory had begun to fray

and a planet drawn and redrawn through
endless shifts of aims and loyalties,
and war and war.

★

Her eye fell at random. "Formosa," she read.
"Now *that's* pretty. Is it there today?"
A pause. "It is," my brother said,

"though now it's called Taiwan."
She looked apologetic. "I sometimes forget . . ."
"Like Sri Lanka," I added. "Which was Ceylon."

And so my brothers and I, globe at hand, began:
which places had seen a change of name
in the last eighty years? Burma, Baluchistan,

Czechoslovakia, Abyssinia, Transjordan, Tibet.
Because she laughed, we extended our game
into history, mist: Vineland, Persia, Cathay . . .

She was in a middle place—
her forties—when photos were first transmitted,
miraculously, from outer space.

Who could believe those men—in their black noon—
got up like robots, wandering the wild
wastelands of the moon,

and overhead a wholly naked sun
and an Earth so far away
it was less real than this one,

the gift received today—
the globe she'd so tenderly fitted
under her arm, like a child.

★

Finally, there's cake: eight candles in a ring.
. . . Just so, the past turns distant past,
each rich decade diminishing

to a little stick of wax, rapidly
expiring. I say, "Now make a wish before
you blow them out." She says, "I don't see—"

stops. Then mildly protests: "But they look so *nice.*"
We laugh at her—and wince when a look of doubt
or fear clouds her face; she needs advice.

Well—what should anyone wish for
in blowing candles out
but that the light might last?

SMALL BUILDING

Ms. Haggerty, in the kitchenette of 1-A,
cleans up last night's mess while listening
to a man in her bedroom, snoring away.

She hardly knows him—his name is Ben—or why
she did what she promised herself she wasn't
going to do again: pick up some guy

at a party and bring him home. Pick up,
then pick up: wine glasses, smeared ice cream bowls,
crab dip, a taco chip afloat in a coffee cup . . .

She relearns her lesson: worse than the one who rolls
out the door soon after he's done, scattering
pet-names and apologies, is the one who doesn't.

★

Although the walls are thin, Ben's snoring
is scarcely loud enough to awaken
old Professor Flyte in 1-B, who's hard of hearing

and is dreaming that his wife, Jill,
is asking him, repeatedly, to walk the dog, old Bard,
out in back of the house until

Bard relieves himself. Even in Flyte's dream there's a dim
sense that *he* needs relief—and it makes him sad,
shuffling to the bathroom, but also amuses him,

to observe that his dream was *triply* mistaken:
it has been many years now since he had
a wife, a dog, or a backyard.

The young man in 2-A rarely goes out
since losing his job. He hasn't found a new living,
but a new life: writing (unpaid, online) reviews about

anything, everything . . . Mukluks. Wood glues.
Local pizzerias that deliver. Competing websites.
Dental floss vs. dental tape. Stand-ups. Microbrews.

A Supreme Court decision . . . He's building a place
for himself; he jokes that his soul's now
homesteading in Cyberspace—

though with an occasional misgiving
that, given the Web's rate of growth, he's somehow
steadily losing ground, however fast he writes.

★

It's how Eliza likes a Saturday:
to be first one up and methodically
haul out the supplies her mother put away

and begin to create—
a word she adores. (Her father smiles
when she uses it.) She's ten, and draws straight

from her imagination one elegantly
gowned, crowned princess after another. It would seem
each new drawing ensures that the girl in 2-B

will become the grown-up she plans to be:
a woman whose face is a dream
and whose legs go for miles.

★

Chandra dreamed of space and elegance but found
something better: a place where people live
just how they want, wandering around

in prison gear, pajamas, dog collars, underwear—
nothing could be too wild.
She came here from Thailand, as an au pair,

to apartment 3-A (and a room surprisingly small),
and she loves the movies, the music, the food, too;
she loves the regular mall and the outlets mall.

She loves *everything* except the child—
red-haired Dougie, who, though recently turned two,
is unreasonable and unappreciative.

★

It's me, in 3-B. Saturdays, I like to do
some early morning vacuuming,
but I must first be careful to

sterilize my hands. I vacuum not the floor
(which is thickly carpeted
with papers, clothes, CDs) but the floor

of my aquarium—a fine gravel bed.
I set up my little kit and rapidly
get the gravel doing a spirited

dance in the siphon tube, whose suctioning
loosens the clinging, greenish debris
in which contagion's bred.

The guppies, mollies, cool glass cats, the hot red
neons—they're my people, you might say. What's more—
it's something I've often said.

A drink in hand, maybe, on nights when I'm alone,
I'll often watch them instead of TV.
They inhabit a small building of their own,

open and contained. They're a flowing,
ceaseless parade of movement, color, appetite—though
inevitably one must ask: Where are they going?

Or even: What's the *point* of life? Generally,
I avoid asking, content to see them so
pretty and well cared for.

★

I read somewhere—I don't know if it's true—
that because goldfish lack short-term memory
the vistas are perpetually new

as they go round and round the bend;
any goldfish bowl is as big as the ocean.
As for what my own fish comprehend,

I know they undergo (although this task of mine
is gently performed) a quick, deep resistance
at trespasses against their domain:

my hand breaks the water, wakes a fierce frenzied motion . . .
They, too, call on guardian angels to oversee
their welfare, and prefer these keep their distance.

UNDERGONE

After his wife left him, he wrote
many mental personal ads ("Young prof on verge
of 60, 6 ft, newly single . . . ," and "Second-rate

academic, few publications
but big heart . . . ," and "M seeks F to heal
his soul . . . ," and "M seeks F for usual relations . . . ,"

and "Man seeks Woman who shares
his passion for marine environment and his
outrage at how nobody apparently cares

that it's all going Straight to Hell")
and sought to resubmerge
himself in his specialty: sea lettuces.

After his wife left him, he found
he'd find himself—having lost all track of time—
steadily pondering the whitecapped sound.

He'd sit in his low-tech, low-cost
prefab office at the lab and watch the sea, while bringing
to mind, with a vividness he'd feared lost,

the diner dinner where she proposed; or their unplanned
first night (aided by the small emergency
of a leaking tent); or the first time he took her hand

(a coastal hike; he'd helped her climb
a boulder's face and, back on the trail, kept clinging
to that hand, as if forgetfully).

After his wife left, he converted her study
into The Next-Week Room. He set up a folding table,
where he laid out his tasks so that anybody

could appraise them: a week's clothes, in daily piles,
a change of towels, a change of bedding,
upcoming lecture notes, relevant business files . . .

He printed up a meal chart
and bought a big old-fashioned wall calendar,
and all of this was good, it was *smart:*

there was genuine comfort in being able
simply to throw open a door
and see where your life was heading.

After his wife left, doors turned out to be
one of two recurring images in his mind's eye.
He could *see* it: how, totally silently,

the knob would start to rotate, and then—then she,
likewise breathless, would slip through the door . . .
    The other image was drawn from the sea:

the way a diver loses colors, serially,
reds first (at twenty feet or so),
yellows, greens, at last blues. That's what he'd see:

Earth's deepest blue, easing to black, by and by,
in that journey all sea-dwellers undergo
to the lightless lost-and-found of the ocean floor.

MOON OVER

Scuba divers will sometimes drown
within a night sea
after confusing up and down.

It seems so *basic*—up/down—and yet,
immersed in a black neutral buoyancy,
the world's boundaries all wet,

a person may mislay his only meaningful
compass—the heart in his head—
and mistake Earth's centripetal pull

for that other mustering of gravity:
a firmament widespread
with stars, over a wind blowing free.

★

But the figure—the tiny figure floundering,
lost, in an unlit sea . . . He's trapped
like a sleeper trapped in a raw, tightening

nightmare, who knows he knows a way out of here
though he keeps forgetting
the key.
                How do we wake? How do we clear

the borne mind of its body and arrive—
gasping, half gone, not gone—
on the surface's groundless shore, not just alive

but secure in the moon's artful netting,
whose catch tonight may be one of those rapt
souls that thinks to see another dawn?

THE OTHER SIDE

The sun never knew how great it was
until it hit the side of a building.
LOUIS KAHN

. . . Nor was the moon the moon,
before at last it fell
on the prospect of a ruin.

Decades, centuries—until one night
the assembled workings of the day
shiver in a spill of moonlight,

as the first presumptive fissure
on the glittering palace wall
sings like a signature.

Lunar writ. Or call it a silver spell
of time—commingling delay
and decay while claiming one and all.

★

. . . Or a moon raking over old ground—
Mayan jungle. A jungle moon, bent
on scrutinizing each teeming, cryptic mound

for traces of the shapes and ways
of a smothered civilization.
It's a moon of another phase—

a restorative moon, which glories
in exhuming, for one, the open-air
terraced observatories

of lost priests who looked nowhere
save to the riddled firmament
for the secrets of preservation.

BAD BREAKS

I. Jen and Jason, 2007

One morning she mentioned not liking his tattoo.
—All right, truth was, he didn't like *hers*.
—Right, but *hers* wasn't right out in plain view.

—Right, but wasn't that the point: who'd
want to see one *there*? —Well, he ought to know
the truth: it was revolting, how he chewed his food.

—Did *he* suck up to teachers? —*And* clothes you'd wear in prison.
—So how long was she keeping this list of his crimes?
. . . It was amazing, really: the grievances arisen

in a mere two months. After two hours'
arguing, neither could recall *ever* wanting to go
to bed with the other. Let alone, so many times.

II. Louie and Christopher, 1998

They'd weathered rough patches in the past,
and it looked as if they might do so again,
until the endless dinner party where Louie at last

told a tale of taking a five-mile jog one day
up in Maine and eventually discovering
he'd been pursued the entire way

by Christopher—no runner, heaven knows . . .
"He could've died! And just *who* was he thinking I
might be—trysting with? [Laughter.] A moose, I suppose.

[More laughter.] I ask you, what's to be done with a guy
so crazy-blind with jealousy?" Not a thing.
Because next day he was gone.

III. Gerry and Sally, 1984

As everyone who ought to know knew,
he was a bang-up litigator, with a keen legal eye
(and a former editor of his law review),

and yet it wasn't until his twenty-fourth year
of married life (discussing an overdue
gas bill, of all things) it suddenly grew clear

one day that Sally's standard argument
at bottom was, "The reality
of the situation isn't what's relevant,

sweetie—what's relevant is my
response to it, can't you see?"
and he saw he was through.

IV. Ron and Barb, 1978

It was the too calm way
her husband-the-science-teacher
got out the torn sheet and wrapped up old Desiree,

saying nothing. No, it was the notion that he'd
settled on his plan without ever
consulting her: the dog would be autopsied.

No, it was the realization that just because
she'd disliked the filthy thing—shedding everywhere—
she now lay under suspicion. No, it was

the recurring image of their poking their
instruments into that ancient creature,
probing for murder, that meant her marriage was over.

V. XX and XY, 1952

First the little creature had to swim an ocean,
repeatedly, then succeed in finding
the remote mother ship, itself in motion,

then, for all her impregnable hull, contrive a way
to board her. Which it did. Yes, the infinitesimal
creature, wielding a select chemical array

of secretions, pierced both the corona
radiata and, in an ejaculate's ejaculation—
a spray of enzymes from the sperm head—the zona

pellucida. And then: a climactic binding
of membranes, and an eventual
fusion with the oocyte. Or two became one.

And then it was all
a matter of paradoxical increase-through-
division—an exponential,

not yet visible aggregating. It was all
about quickly attaining a size
where replication might support radical

differentiation, and a primitive animal,
enveloped in a round, lightless sea,
be intricately outfitted for an unimaginable

displacement—bright-angled skies,
grounded panoramas—at the close of an odyssey
from cell to self. Or one becomes two.

The body's permanent ink is blood—
this time spilled between the legs, an unforeseen,
breaking flow that rapidly became a flood

obliterating everything
she and her husband so dearly coveted.
Later, they both lay sobbing, whimpering.

Later, she wept alone—her tears, too, an unstoppable flow.
She'd gone, this time, four weeks later (before she miscarried),
and this time she couldn't let it—her child—go.

For she'd felt it *as* a child, a live spirit buried
in blood, in flushed water—and nothing anybody said
could blunt the horrors of that cleansed final scene.

She'd felt it—as her boy: she had no doubt
about its sex. And from that crux her imagination
could take flight—hair, eyes, voice—filling out

the details of his humanity.
                              It's not the not
knowing but the never knowing—the lost *could be*—
that turns the world so cruel and unfortunate.

Who's to say he wasn't the new Michelangelo?
Or a Mozart? *Who could say?* There was no telling . . .
Surely, it happens all the time: Michelangelos go

missing, Mozarts never pen a note—a notion
dismissible as wildly romantic if, mathematically,
it were not so compelling.

She felt it bitterly: the task of weeping was now hers alone.
 . . . Yet there were odd, dislocating interludes when
she observed things from some variant zone—

seeing herself outside herself—and then she knew
that this person she'd chosen to live beside,
her husband, was doing everything a soul could do.

Still, she couldn't bear—for weeks and weeks—his touch,
until a night she looked at him (once more, from far away)
and read upon his face not desire so much

as an old human willingness to concede
all defeat but final defeat, and heard him say,
"Darling, let's try again."

A VASE

There was a vase
that held the world's riches, but it wasn't cheap.
It cost a dime—and this in a time and place

when dimes were sizable, especially for
a girl of eight whose construction-worker father
was unemployed. The old metaphor

was literal in this case and she
counted her pennies till there were ten—
then embarked on a mission of great secrecy,

a purchase whose joys ran so deep,
seventy years later, as she told the tale again,
her face flushed. It was a birthday gift for her mother.

There was a race
of people heretofore glimpsed only on hanging scrolls
in library books. They were on the vase—

the smallest whole figures imaginable,
purposeful and industrious
as they fished or planted rice or hiked a hill

whose spiral trail led to a temple perched upon
a crag between cloud and waterfall.
They were a vision exported from Japan—

a country far as the moon, and far more beautiful,
whose artists grasped an eight-year-old girl's soul's
need for the minutely amplitudinous.

There was a place
(Detroit, the thirties) now slipped from sight,
though here and there I'll catch some hold-over trace—

maybe the grille on an old apartment door,
or a slumped block of houses, draped
in torn sheets of rain, apparently posing for

black-and-white photographs. Even the out-
of-a-job, men like my grandfather, donned hats back then
before leaving the house—to circle endlessly about,

as if a lost job were a lost coin that might
yet be found on the street where it had been dropped,
making them whole again.

There was a face,
rucked with care, that would dreamily soften
if talk floated off toward some remote someplace

beyond the seas. My grandmother had a yen for the faraway
(which she imparted to her daughter),
even as her life was tethered between a gray

icy motionless Midwestern city—
stalled like a car with a frozen ignition—
and a Tennessee farm without electricity.

(She did once see Washington—cherry season—and often
spoke of those long pink walkways beside the water
that were Japan's gift to a grateful nation.)

There is a vase—
a piece of gimcrack that somehow
made its way to a crowded curio case

in a small souvenir shop
in Detroit, seventy-plus years ago—
which today stands atop

the mantel in the apartment in D.C.
where my fading mother is now living.
When she was eight, in 1933,

she gave it to my grandmother, who
for all her poverty bequeathed her daughter so
rich a bounty, including a taste for giving:

the gift of grace.
It seems a little miracle
almost—that it's intact, the little vase,

conveying what its makers set out to convey:
an inward island spared by Time,
by the times. These days, she can scarcely say

who she gave it to, or on what occasion.
A—birthday? The pilgrim climbs the winding hill
forever, station by station,

and "Isn't it beautiful?"
she asks. "You bought it for a dime,"
I tell her. It holds the world's riches still.

II. VARIABLE WEATHER

SLEEPING THROUGH A BLIZZARD

(Thingvellir, Iceland)

9 p.m.

This wind seems hell-bent
On fleeing the scene of some
Distant accident.

11 p.m.

The cracked pane restrings
A web wherein some dark winged
Thing sings for its life.

1 a.m.

The bending storm blows
Out the stars, makes a wish: Let
Blackness alone blaze.

5 a.m.

The storm writes its o-
verheated rage in the snow
Before letting go.

SLEEPING BY THE SHORE

(Kilifi, Kenya)

Breakers

The sea is airing
Rumors of a dark morning
In a slow murmur.

A Cricket

The bright needle sings
As each black haystack ransacks
Itself on the beach.

Bigger Breakers

Out of the roaring
Smithy come long arms bearing
Fistfuls of trinkets.

Beyond the Reef

The moon's old rope-bridge
Over the sea? Too frayed, now,
For human passage.

REMOTE MIDNIGHTS

Icelandic Mouse

As, safe in its hole,
The field mouse quakes when the hawk
Soars across the sky,
So the candle, indoors, shakes
When the wind goes howling by.

Kenyan Lion

. . . The leaves, too, quiver
At the roar of a creature
Whose gullet's vaster
Than that lair where the battered
Blood-streaming sun's retreated.

DISTANT DAWNS

Iceland

My fire will run out
Of coal before the blizzard
Falls short of snowflakes.
Only the scuttle of dreams
Could shortfall the difference.

Kenya

Not even if all
The night's spare moon- and star-light
Were salted away
In the ocean's vault could we
Account for such a return.

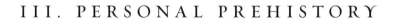

III. PERSONAL PREHISTORY

THE BIRTH OF INJUSTICE

Meandering Neandertals
keep bumping up against

the glacier's high, invasive walls,
whose blackened snout

comes down to eat
the ground underneath their feet.

Which is the way now?
What else but hunched despair's

narrowing valleys, this gathering
feeling of everything

constricting?
              It's an old notion, nearly sensed
from way back when: somehow,

this exorbitant venture of theirs
—Life—isn't working out.

She's a brooder, this one,
on her rock, who once or twice, or thrice

(no words for numbers yet),
has laid a child to earth. They take

the tiny body from your arms and it goes
down into a cold mouth we make

ourselves, digging out the shape.
                                    The ice
eats, the earth eats, and having set

her haunches on a rock, she ponders the light:
it's dawn, or dusk, no language for

origins or ends, and yet the sun
is moving, and in her blood she knows

always their dwindling journey has been far
too brutal: something's not right.

This big-boned figure who
subsists chiefly on cattails she prises

from the numb gray sand
of a half-frozen pond

prefers of course
the soft and steamy organs of horse

or aurochs, when those are in hand—
not often enough.
                        Not often enough, days

warmly warm, all the way through,
when the wished sun rises

up in your chest with the blaze
of honey on the tongue, for you the ache

and sting of it, sweet beyond
any sounds a mouth might make.

EARLIER

The philologist's reply was *utu e ta;*
naturally, I asked him to repeat it. "*Utu*

e ta. Sumerian. Not really my line.
But so far as I know, the oldest word for dawn

in any attested language."
                                        Well, what do you say
to that? Naturally, the table fell

silent, except for a neat clinking
of spoons; we were eating crème brulée.

A dinner party in Washington. Late fall.
Conversation winding down.

Some of the guests were drinking
coffee, some of us the last of the wine.

"Think of that. It's quite a thought,"
our hostess said. "The oldest dawn." Yes, think of that . . .

Weeks later, I give the word a try,
murmuring the syllables while seated

beside a window in a café
in Reykjavik, that city of arctic nights

in dire need of dawns—nearly noon, and the sun
a mere rumor.
                        Quite a cosmopolitan scene,

even so. At a table nearby,
two Japanese businessmen share a heated

exchange—come to purchase fish, maybe, or fishing rights.
Lord knows what led the five Spaniards here, or

what indeed the low-toned Icelanders are looking for.
It's morning anyway, in a way,

and strong coffee flows. And words flow.
We're in the present—today's today—and the words go.

Paleolinguists, crouched upon the ancient Hill
of Speech, sift the strata of generations

of buried chatter, laboring to unearth
ever earlier ur-formations:

a sound that once gave birth
to a sound that gave birth to a sound

the rest of us can identify . . .
Dead languages speak to others, deader still;

the past expands, while going underground.
In truth, everything, always, seems to be making

a passage back to that flaired moment when,
                                        as one
more day was soundlessly breaking

across the heavens, a signifying cry
rose from a human throat and colonized the sun.

AN ALL BUT EMPTY SET

He or she was hard-wired
to calculate

in nanoseconds, light-years; to climb
summit to summit above

the squat mud settlements, and oversee
the pyramid poised on pyramid

of exponents stacked exponentially;
even to intrapolate

the condensed hadal incandescence of
the raging substrata of the sun.

For this was Earth's first math prodigy, who made
but one solitary error, in time,

allying his gift to a species that had no word
as yet for three, for two, for one . . .

Antedating words, out-deepening words—the recognition
of pattern, repetition, a feel of design.

Sometimes it snows.
Sometimes it doesn't. Sometimes everything

shifts forward, back. The river overflows
the bank sometimes, depositing a mark, a sign.

Clouds assemble, they disassemble.
Watch for: marks, signs. Watch: wind in the ferns. Rain

on the sand, pattering, patterning.
A snapped branch weeps, rich

resins, and we divine a world through want, and pain,
and a murked, associative notion—

vast as a teardrop, in which
sun and moon, dependent, tremble.

In Halle, Germany, somewhat later,
(a few eye-blinks later, a tiny shifting

of clouds later—but sufficient for the surfacing
of calendars, colleges), a nineteenth-century

professor, Georg Cantor, forever drifting
in and out of sanatoria, witnessed the set of real

numbers surpassing the naturals (it would seem
one limitless thing might out-reach another limitless thing).

And the firmament, sunder-struck, was riven to reveal
ascending orders of boundlessness, one greater

than the next, infinite diversity
of infinities, with One overseeing, conceiving all,

for Whom our globe's a clay particle,
and the sun a backlit bubble on a stream.

It's a hunger that finds no way—none—
to sate itself; you gaze and gaze, into the distance,

clouds presaging circles, angles, lines,
but no sound-shapes for circle, angle, line . . . They fascinate,

nonetheless, the dog-eager clouds, who fill and flow
and go, lunge and long, so like the designs

in your head, nights, storms, the unspun fantasy
of shelter opening on an otherworldly scale,

immenser than any cave, exclusively
lit by the constellations of the inner skull.

You walk erect beneath them. It's home. You have no
home, but here you'd have it, were there one.

Were there one, you'd choose a variant existence,
but you have no choice: you choose to wait.

LONG ODDS

Chances are good
it's the world's oldest pair of dice, though

the adjacent card in the museum case
hedges all bets with a *possibly.*

But shake it off—all doubt—and heed the glow
of good fortune: these little blocks of wood

(presumably hewn from the same tree,
their pips mostly worn away),

bounced and bounded and spun
across an obstacle race

that left all the others behind.
The course was long and hazardous—designed

to lay players no less than tools of play
to rest, dust to dust, dice to dust—and they have won.

. . . although it's far from clear
what winning connotes for those

unaware of their appointed game—unaware of all
games and players. The competition here

was among little wood blocks and small
terra cotta cubes, or among (accessories

to a larger game) arrowheads, axeheads, tent
stakes, hides, whittled batons, bone fragments, bowl

fragments, rags, gourds, cords . . . Hence it's left to us
to take what's left to us

after sifting the flung sediment
of our hunched excavations and to impose

a pattern, a game for which we're the sole
spectators as well as referees.

There never was a throw that ended
interestingly. A pair of dice? Eleven sums within

a mere twenty-one configurations—
that's all. What could the result be

except a bore? Yet to the true gambler, the soul
for whom everything's always riding

upon the very next roll,
it's . . . different as the dice are tumbling. Then,

and only then (all laws of necessity suspended,
heaven's every angle dancing on the head of the spin),

a player might catch intimations
beyond mortal reckoning: the moment when

the universe, choosing its number, bares a deciding
will, partial and unforeseeable and free.

Begin with the four letters of the gene-
alphabet and throw in something like a single die . . .

That's all it takes: a raw capacity
for writing, and a certain somersaulting

summing—call it chance inspiration.
A letter; add a letter; add a letter; and if most fail

to cohere into syllables (one combination
after another that doesn't mean

anything, a babble towering skyward like a tomb),
such disappointments hardly signify.

We've simply to wait. Eventually—
Ages, eons—Mother Nature will unveil

a sonnet, one by one the bright words vaulting
out of the dice-cup womb of time.

Possibly (as our museum curator would say),
these dice had an extended run

in the marketplace, performing
their fore-cast function of getting things

moving—getting the goods into play.
What was wagered? Barley, maybe. Or wine. A bold

moon-mesmerized opal. Philters. A string of black
pearls. Mother-of-pearl. Tiny bracelet bells.

A stout songbird with clipped wings.
A magnetic rock, a straw-coated cheese. A sack

of green-gold apricots; or the pure gold
stacked in a honeycomb's six-sided cells—

plunder won in the great swarming
gambling den of the sun.

THE HORSE IN THE GALLERY

Not to the swift,
but perhaps to the big and strong . . .

The winner of the final race?
Burly equus, the sole finisher.

And the others—what of them?
Lean orohippus, whose long

hind legs suggest a gift
for leaping? Or hippidium,

who took to the hard ground
of the arid high plains? Or

the firstborn and favorite son,
lithe little eohippus, who used to run

on a splayed foot's four toes, round and round
Earth's track of years? Gone. They did not place.

About the size
of a horse—what's to be said

about the size of a horse? Spirited
eohippus, our *horse of the dawn,*

stood less than two feet tall
at its stalwart shoulder—so low,

a readying child must crouch to go
face to face with the delicate brown

skeleton in the old museum hall
whose cloudy cases appear to share

a dust of years' standing.
                        As if in prayer,
our child must kneel down

to get inside the head of the doll-
sized renegade whose eyes

assimilated an amazing
run of worlds now largely lost. Of course

we've read about such worlds, painstakingly
deciphering the scattered image-words

in the volume wherein we live—*Earth's Big Book of Life*—
where epic chiliads may be

compacted in a ghostly stone band
narrower even than a single leaf

of paper.
             You kneel by the child and,
squinting through a snouted skull the size

of a fist, descry the proto-horse
at last, ranged in mindful, diminutive herds

along a riverbank. There they are—grazing.
One lifts its head. You meet its eyes.

This is the closest thing
we have to an eternal flame—

the match-head glance that flares and brightens
as it catches a glance, catches a glance,

and catches a glance, flickering
down through the centuries . . .

Rembrandt painted a rare old bird
of a woman (Margaretha de Geer by name),

who was eighty if a day,
and who even now, alighted among titans

in London's National Gallery, enjoys the last word.
Her look says, Regard me. And we do. For she's

as alive as we. At least. A quick soul glints
through drooping eyes that never look away.

To catch a glance
Of an intensity you can't quite countenance—

What more can we ask of the art
of painter or paleontologist

than these contrivances of ways
to compound and complicate

our evolving sight? What more can you ask for
than a glance that asks for more

than you've actually got the heart
to give? However long you contemplate

Vrouw Geer, when you turn your back
on her, you feel remiss—unjust.

Behind you, a fixed gaze
steadfastly burns. She implores you to turn back.

On legs thin as pencils they ran across
a fresh-drawn landscape. They ran from rise to rise.

Over swales and savannahs. Over moss-
backed bogs and marshes. They ran through thunder and drought.

Born to the forest, they were beginning
to expand operations . . . A race was on—through

gullies, valleys, cloud-cast meadows—and they were winning.
They ran over raw, eroding watersheds

and scrapheaps of scree. Ran through mist, and moonlight.
They were a new design among a slew

of new designs, and they ran their hearts out
and kept running. Scrubland. Salt-slough. Drying riverbeds

whose pebbles, each pigment bright
with hunger, shone back in their eyes.

LITTLE DIG

Others found the bone.
Others identified it. But we'll

play a small part, my daughter and I,
in its phased pilgrimage from

rubbled hillside to museum.
We've each got a hammer in a fist,

and under the sidelong scrutiny
of the predictably bearded paleontologist

who runs the site, we're breaking stone.
. . . The sun is hammering all the while.

It's a hundred degrees in the shade,
if there were any shade

on this bare and baking hill, and we
are breaking stone. Montana. Hell Creek. July.

Others identified the bone
as a triceratops scapula. *If you say so . . .*

It's three feet long, at least,
and a richer brown than the hill's exhausted brown.

Apparently, the creature last
lay down some eighty million years ago—

upon which, the planet's consuming processes
of transformation could begin. Seas

sallied off, valleys buckled. Huge hills lay down.
Even the bones were too soft—they turned to stone.

(As for the flesh, the fernlike splay
of nerves, the susceptible jelly of the eye—

such things vanished utterly, or better say
they dissolved into the sky.)

We're drinking water by the quart,
but we're dissolving too—or just melting away.

It gets hotter still. Salt-sweat rivulets spill
into our eyes, burn—blur. We keep hammering.

Hilary's fifteen, but a good sport.
(Dad wanted to go on a real dig.

Well, we're really digging.) Eventually,
when the bone's free and clear,

we'll wrap it in a plaster cast too big
and heavy to be shouldered out of here.

Weeks after we're gone, a clamoring
helicopter will come and haul it from the hill.

Something we'd love to see: the day
our triceratops takes wing.

The heat climbs back on itself, swaying
like a tower overhead. Its blinding height

induces slow hallucinations, and in time the bone
before me is re-identified, as my own.

My daughter digs it up. Which is right—her birth-
right. It's what a child does: uncovers her parents.

It's what we children do: uncover the past.
In my enfevered head, an image rises—so

hazy you couldn't call it a vision—of a vast
and scattered crowd of souls, uniformly crouched low

upon an endless hill. They have the appearance
of supplicants, but they're not praying—

they're digging. It's what we do: unearth,
unearth . . . To bring the departed to light.

A helicopter will be coming . . . And could there
possibly be any more dramatic

deus ex machina than this?
The term's coiners would have felt terrified—

terrified and confirmed, too,
standing stunned among hills as a colossal bird

reifies thundering out of the blue,
slowly to hoist heavenward

the buried forebear whose long metamorphosis
was meted out within a mountainside.

One moment, the whole hangs clear: our visceral need
for miracles, the hoarse, ecstatic

cries of confirmation—then the craft lifts and leaves the air
emptied of all but echoes. Godspeed.

ALTAMIRA

This particular species of Prospero
is named Sautuola. And the young girl who's

opening in Altamira as Miranda is his
actual daughter, happily

called Maria. The year: 1879.
Setting: a Spanish cave, where—a student of prehistory—

Sautuola digs for axeheads, potsherds.
"Look, Papa! Oxen!"
His gaze climbs—or is he dreaming?

Overhead, *right there,* not oxen but—soaring herds
of horses . . . His breath goes out. O dearest Lord, O brave

old world, that had such creatures in it!—the broken line
of woolly rhino and aurochs and ibex, teeming

congresses that vanished, rumblingly, into one cave
or another, some twenty thousand years ago.

One theory traces the origins
of art to animal masks and crouching hunters who

snuck up on their prey. Created
as tools, the masks evolved, eventually,

into mustering symbols—of potency,
of abstraction, of the gluttings in dissimulated

action—and from there (but a dark step or two)
into airy menageries on the walls above

an ill-clad, shivering visionary's head . . .
Art's born with a starveling's impulse to punch a spear

into the ribs of a big plump creature and to hear
its torn, thrilling squeal of mortal distress; it begins

in dreamt-of spillings of pools of
the world's most arresting pigment: blood-red.

Another theory locates the genesis
of art in balked desire,

the quarry you can't catch up with, quite—
thereby linking the cave-clan in its hillside hole,

sheltered under a ceiling
of dancing abundances of game,

to Titian as he documents the plight
of Actaeon (brought low by an Artemis

whose nakedness animals and women alone may see),
or to the nameless painter, goal much the same,

who teased out the creature (surprised in dishabille—
witness the breast's blushing aureole)

sheltered within the peeling
cigar box lid: fairest phantom of smoke and fire . . .

Still another: art was at first a sort of prop
for the polyglot shaman for whom

it served as glimmering backdrop.
The flying horses were but the train

of the oracle's arrival, whose cadences spoke
from the unsounded gut of crag and brook,

cloudbank and lightning stroke.
    . . . Today, the caves are like the dressing room

of some nightclub magician on his dinner break—
having left behind, in limp disarray,

silk scarves, a rope, a cape, a cane,
decks of cards, false-bottomed boxes, a top

hat with a false top, tinted powders, a bouquet
of plastic flowers, a two-headed coin.

As for our play? The action shifts to another ancient hill
and cave: Lascaux. A second Spaniard appears

on stage, looking truly humbled (humbled but bold—
he is Picasso, after all) as he observes,

"We've learned nothing in twelve thousand years."
Behind him, the whisperings of an unseen river.

    . . . This master-draftsman, renowned for having gone
back to the dim nubs, the prised angles and curves

of classical statuary, flickers with the light
of something older, newer still.

The deep eyes flame in the bald
dome of his skull, as well they might,

having glimpsed once more the leap of art forever
figuring its way to an earlier dawn.

Hundreds of Fireflies

DUCKWEED

Where there was a pond there's
Now a floating carpet,
   Gold-butter-green,
   And smooth as pond water.
      The carpet shares

With those extensive, spare
Cumulus plains one sees by plane
   A false firmness—
   As if only step lightly
      And it would bear

Your weight; cloud-false, too,
In its suggestion
   Of indwelling light, some
   Deep-deposited radiance.
      Only if you

Kneel to scrutinize
Its surface closely
   Will you begin to see
   How many mini-lily pads
      Of brad's-head size

Were needed to transform
The shadowed pool
   Through emanant domain.
   But dip your hands to part
      The duckweed's warm

Sealing, and here's
A room below: uninviting
By nature, and one—chill,
Dim, jumbled—nobody's
Entered for years.

AN EXPANDED WANT AD

Rent—cttge Pig Riv
3 bdrm stove fridge
20 acr—lovely view

Although it's true
a few screens are torn and various
uninvited types may flutter through,
    some of them to bite you,

    and true the floors
buckle and sag like a garden plowed
by moles, which makes the shaky chairs
    seem shakier, and the bedroom doors

    refuse to close
(you'll have three bright bedrooms—and a fine
kitchen, a living room with fireplace,
    and bath with shower hose),

    there's a good view
of the Pigeon, a river that carries
more than its share of sunny jewelry,
    for days here are mostly blue,

    and nights so clear
and deep that in a roadside puddle
you can spot the wobbly flashlight flare
    of even a minuscule star.

    The jolting road,
two muddy ruts, flanks a weedy fan
that slithers against the underside
    of a car, then rises unbowed,

but better still,
go on foot—though this means mosquitoes—
and stop at the overgrown sawmill,
   with its fragrant wood-chip pile,

and, stooping, enter
that shack the length of a compact car
where two loggers outbraved the bitter
   sting of a Michigan winter.

The room is dim,
spider-strung; you'll sense the whittled lives
they led—how plain, pure, and coldly grim
   the long months were to them . . .

Just a short ways
up the road you'll come to a birch clump
which on all overcast mornings glows
   with a cumulus whiteness

and in the brief
light after sunset holds a comely
allusive blush—a mix that's one half
   modesty, the other mischief.

While if you hike
to where the road feeds a wider road
you'll find a mailbox above a choke
   of weeds, leaning on its stake;

it looks disowned,
worthless, but will keep your letters dry
though its broken door trails to the ground
   like the tongue of a panting hound.

Venture across
this wider road to reach a pasture,
whose three horses confirm that "the grass
    is always greener" applies

to them as well:
offered shoots from your side of the fence,
they'll joggle forward to inhale
    a verdant airy handful,

and will emit
low shivering snorts of joy, and will—
while you feed them—show no appetite
    for the grass growing at their feet.

Now, it may happen
the first nights you'll feel an odd unease,
not lessened by the moths' crazed tapping
    at the glass; and later, sleeping

unsteadily,
as bullfrogs hurl harsh gravelly notes
from slingshot throats, you may wonder why
    you ever left the city.

Should this occur,
think of the creatures you've not yet glimpsed,
the owl and woodchuck and tense-necked deer
    you'll meet if you remain here;

remember, too,
morning's flashy gift—for when day breaks
it mends all wrongs by offering you
    drenched fields, nearly drowned in dew.

MINIATURE

Beneath lilac clusters on a plain
two feet by two, two
long-necked dandelions sway
over a toiling community;
grain by grain,

coppery skin
blazing as if sweat-painted,
· the ants amass a sort of pyramid
on Mayan lines: broad
base and truncated cone.

One dandelion
is yellow, is a solar flame
spoking from a green nether rim;
the other gray, a dainty crumb-
cake of a moon.

Soon gusts will shake
this moon and it—no moon at all—
detach a drifting astral
scatter; no sun, the sun cool
and blanch and wear a lunar look;

but under weighted air, noon's
dominion, laborers erect a temple
to this sun and moon, unable
to compass decay, indeed unmindful
of all suns and moons.

BETWEEN LEAPS

Binoculars I'd meant for birds
catch instead, and place an arm's length away,
        a frog
compactly perched on a log that lies
    half in, half out of the river.

He may be preying, tongue wound to strike,
but to judge from his look of grave languor
        he seems
to be sunning merely. His skin gleams with light
    coming, rebuffed, off the water; his back's

tawny-spotted, like an elderly hand,
but flank's the crisp, projecting green
        of new
leafage, as if what ran through his veins
    was chlorophyll and he'd

tapped that vegetal sorcery
which, making light of physical bounds,
        makes food
of light. Given the amplitude of his
    special greenness, it requires no large hop

of imagination to see him as
the downed trunk's surviving outlet, from which,
        perhaps,
dragged-out years of collapsing roots
    may prove reversible. With a reflection-

shattering *plop*, a momentary
outbreak of topical, enlarging rings
that chase
one another frenziedly, the place's spell
is lifted: the trunk bare, the frog elsewhere.

11 ASTRONOMICAL RIDDLES

i. The Sun

I am a blinding eye.
I will never relent.
I am magnificent.

I dare them to try.
They hide in the black.
Afraid to attack.

ii. Mercury

I huddle closest to the heat
    Yet my back is cold
As ice. I am the most fleet,
    If the least bold.

iii. Venus

I am tempestuous, hot and cloudy.
    I pay no mind.
Love was intended to be rowdy,
    Torrid and blind.

iv. Earth's Moon

I'm an aging beauty, unique because
It is night not day that betrays my flaws.

v. Earth

I am the spry little
Cell. I am the riddle
Of the chicken or the egg, the miracle of birth.
But for me, none in the heavens would have any worth.

vi. Mars

Chill, frail, friendly . . . I've been misunderstood:
My color shows a love of warmth, not blood.

vii. Jupiter

The vastest and best am I, the eldest son.
Son in one sense if not the other one . . .
Yet I will be king when his day is done.

viii. An Asteroid

Small, I turn with the great. I feel the same
Call of gravity, though I have no name.

ix. Saturn

Too pretty a ring steals praise from its hand,
Unless the hand be fair enough to wear it.

Around my throat I hook an ivory band.
True beauty is bold; I know my own merit.

x. Uranus and Neptune

We're twins, big-boned boys, pale and overweight.
You mustn't criticize us if we're late.
    It's hard for us to run.
A single lap is an enormous length.
We try not to think, to conserve our strength.
    Sleeping is the most fun.

xi. Pluto

All the others look in; I out.
All the others believe; I doubt.
I stand at the gate of unending Night,
    My fingers on the handle.
Who, when they could have uncountable Light,
    Would settle for a candle?

TWO SUMMER JOBS

I. Tennis Instructor, 1971

Transformed: the high school graduate, now
himself a teacher for the city.
Not sure who my students are, or how
exactly a tennis class is run,
I show up an hour ahead of time.
Odd: nobody here. But one by one
they appear and—and they're all women!
Maddeningly shy, the truth is I'm
more alarmed than pleased at this, although
a number of them are pretty,
and one, Mrs. Shores, extremely so.

Mine's a small yet adequate domain.
Three mornings a week I hold court
on two courts beside the railroad track—
giving, to those I can, assistance,
and verbally patting on the back
the irretrievably maladroit
whose shots are always rocketing
the fence. Occasionally a train
hurtling to or from Detroit
rumbles through, erasing everything
before it fades into the distance.

Distant but surreally vast,
exclusive, quick to take offense,
the "Big H," Harvard, which only last
April accepted me, now conspires
(my latest crazy daydream runs)
to bar me from settling in a dorm
because I typed "No class presidents,
please" on my roommate selection form.

Just as I'm lunging toward the ball,
a sniping voice within inquires,
"What will happen in the fall?"

The days are changeless, but the weeks pass,
edging me closer to fall, and school.
Mrs. Shores, the day of our last class,
gives a party on her patio,
where I'm handed a glass-bottom mug
—surprise!—engraved with my name.
Beer's offered; I'm too proud to confess
I hate the stuff. It's hot as a blow-
torch now, and not yet noon. The first slug
of Stroh's goes down in a cool
wash of cleansing bitterness.

The party warms up, visibly. Ice
crackles in the drinks. I'm nonplussed
when Mrs. Binstock unfolds a tale
which—though nothing you shouldn't say
among men—is not exactly nice.
My face, which lets me down without fail
at such times, blushes. They laugh at me.
Then, and this is odd, I am discussed
in a fond but distant-seeming way,
as if I were no longer here.
The ghost accepts another beer.

Mrs. Dow speaks of a friend's friend's son
who committed suicide after
his first Harvard exam. A lighter
flares beside me, and cigarette smoke
crowds the air. "Teacher don't allow
any smoking." Freshened laughter
greets sad Mrs. Klein's unlikely quip.
Then, from Mrs. Shores: "What kind of writer
do you want to be?" How, how, how

did she ever draw from me my one
most private wish? I'm tempted to joke,

but a stilled politeness in the air
and the depths of her dark handsome eyes
forbid it. Yet when I stumblingly
begin a pained, self-conscious reply
she is mercifully there
to cut me off; conversation drifts
lightly away, as once more I
find myself taking shelter in
something that soothes as it puzzles me—
a solicitude that's graceful, wise,
and impenetrably feminine.

I drain my mug. A white film adheres
to the glass bottom, and then bursts:
disclosing these my students seated
around me in the Michigan sun,
the last of our lessons completed.
Wobbly I rise, drunk with success
(successfully having drunk four beers!),
and wave goodbye—but forget the press
to my racket. I'm called back amid
much laughter. Once more I gravely bid
them all farewell: So long. It's been fun.

. . . And what a day this is! The air
humming in my ears, the sun stroking
overheads in the treetops! Now
a second film breaks, revealing how
the light-drinking leaves, the houses, cars,
power lines, a peeling wooden fence
and the pavement's constellated stars
are a network, supple and immense,
and all linked to distant Mrs. Shores,
who calls—but surely she is joking—
"Never forget: the world is yours."

II. Law Clerk, 1979

My fingers having checked and re-checked my tie,
I'm at ease—or nearly so. We're lunching high
over Manhattan, a hundred floors above
streets new to me still. He asks whether I

find the work "exciting." Behind him a buffet
tastefully boasting shrimp, squid salad, paté,
beef, chicken, cheeses, and some good marinated
mushrooms calls me to come boyishly away

and fill my plate a second time. And I'd love
another beer. I think he thinks that one's enough.
"Exciting? Very"—which is not untrue.
"Best of all"—I'm speaking off the (starchy) cuff—

"I liked the document search in Tennessee."
Indeed, I did. How strange, how fine to be
a someone someone flies a thousand miles
to analyze ancient business files! Now he—

but who is he? A *partner,* first of all,
by which is meant no confederate or pal
of mine, but a star in the firm's firmament.
He's kind, though, funny, and lunch is going well

enough—the conversation light, the view vast
beyond my farthest hopes. The kid's arrived at last:
not just New York, but New York at the top.
Just think of all the noontime views that passed

into the void because I wasn't here! Think
of the elevated wines I never drank
in this very room! The tortes I failed to eat!
—Lunch here is money in the memory bank.

Why, then, wishing I were somewhere else? Why
does my glance drift sidelongingly, my mind stray
from his fatherly banter? When will I shake
this shakiness? It's worse at night. I sometimes stay

late at the office. The place starts thinning out
by six; cleaning women, outfitted to fight
their bosses' daily disarray, marshal vacuums,
trashbins, brooms. Their leaving leaves me free to write,

or to try, as the city underfoot
starts breathing visibly, bubbles of light,
hundreds and hundreds, a champagne glitter
promising love and—more—a distant, delicate

loveliness. *Here* is inspiration. Yet the clock
clicks; my mind does not. Could this be "writer's block,"
nothing but that ailment which, like tennis elbow,
raises its victim's status? Yet it's no joke,

this scooped-out feeling, a sense that language
will never span the gap within. The Brooklyn Bridge,
trafficking in cars and literary ghosts,
shimmers mockingly below. I can't budge

the block; thwarted, I inch instead toward parody,
Keats' "On the Grasshopper and Cricket" to be
wittily urbanized as "The Snowplow
and the Lawnmower"; I'll set "The poetry

of earth is never dead" upon its head.
And yet, though I have the title, and the thread
of a joke as a starter's cord, "Snowplow" will not
start: some mechanical failure under the hood.

In a later, hopeless project Shakespeare
writes in a fancy bar—"To beer or not to beer"
and "The Singapore Slings and Sombreros
cost an outrageous fortune." I'm going nowhere . . .

Most nights, the air's sticky. Too hot to jog,
I take myself out for a walk, like a dog,
once round the block. Inside, endlessly, my
electric fan rustles like a paper bag;

and armed with a borrowed book called *Parodies,*
I rifle my old English 10 anthologies
in search of targets. It seemed this would be simple
but it's not. And I'm hot. And the nights pass

slowly. Then: a new month: still stuck, parodies lost,
when, wolfing lamb at lunch, I find I've crossed
Cinderella's fable (a cleaning woman swept
like me into moneyed worlds) with—Robert Frost.

"Whose shoe this is I need to know.
Throughout the countryside I'll go
In search of one whose gaze is clear,
Whose royal skin is white as snow."

Now *this* is simple, stanzas dropping into place,
and while I couldn't say precisely what it is
I'd like to say, just writing quickly is enough.
And the last stanza is, I think, quite nice:

"And if she's lost, I'll settle cheap—
A helpmate from the common heap,
Some kitchenmaid or chimneysweep,
Some kitchenmaid or chimneysweep."

What now?—next? Will the impasse pass? After work,
I'm roundabouting home through Central Park
when a voice cuts short all questions. *"Bradford."*
It sounds like someone I hope it isn't. ". . . Mark."

He's wearing jeans and a work-shirt with a rip
in the neck, whereas I'm caught in the trap-
pings of a Wall Street lawyer. As we lob our
pleasantries across the Sartorial Gap

he studies me. Mark's a poet too, if you take
the thought for the deed—but who am I to talk?
At Harvard, hardly friends, we were nonetheless
drawn together by a fiercely sophomoric

contest: my-potential's-bigger-than-yours.
He's just in for the day, he quickly offers,
as if this were a kind of feat. City living
taints the artist's soul—he's suggesting of course—

which is his old, still tiresome refrain. So why
do I yet feel some need to justify
myself to him, who, he tells me, moved to a farm,
makes pots (a bad sign) and (I'm sure) lives high

on Daddy's bucks. His dad makes pots and pots
of money in securities—but let's
not hear me griping at the rich while wearing
one of my two two-hundred-dollar suits.

Mark draws from a knapsack the books he's bought—
Pound, Lawrence, Durrell (I thought he was out),
Smart and Clare (safer choices, both being mad)
and a surprising, handsome *Rubaiyat*.

Mark asks about my job. He has me twice
repeat my salary, each time bulging his eyes
in sham barefaced amazement. Later, alone
and gleefully free to wage my wars in peace,

I derail a quatrain (striking at that band
of Harvard potters who'd "live off the land"
a summer or two before going on
for M.B.A.'s, just as the parents planned):

"A Book of Verses underneath the Bough,
A Jug of Wine, a Loaf of Bread, and Thou-
sands in the Bank; fleeting though Riches be,
And powerless, They comfort anyhow."

Yes . . . And all at once, summer's nearly through.
I return *Parodies,* a week overdue.
And I'm asked to join the firm, beginning next year,
with four months to decide . . . Oftener now

I linger at work, to watch how the setting sun
at once sharpens and softens the skyline;
sometimes—the better for being rare—the dusk-light's
perfect and, while occupied toy boats twine

the Hudson with long, unraveling wakes,
the sun buffs hundreds of windows, reglazes bricks,
ruddies a plane's belly like a robin's,
and seems to free us from billable time, from stocks

and bonds (both words a pun, ironically,
on hand-fetters), leases, estate taxes, proxy
fights, adverse parties, complainants, claimants,
motions to suppress, to enjoin, to quash, oxy-

moronic lengthy briefs, and the whole courtly game
of claim and counterclaim; seems to say we come
through drudgery to glory . . . Look—down there! Wall
Street's turned to gold at last! And there are some

silver nights of emptied offices, raindrops
washing out the glue on those envelopes
in which memories are sealed and the entire
cleared distances offered up, all the old hopes

intact, as if nothing's been mislaid. This obscure
sense that one's past is safely banked somewhere
finds confirmation each time the recumbent
city, touched by darkness, begins to stir

and with a sufferance that's nearly heartbreaking
undergoes a pane by pane awakening
until just as fresh, as sparklingly replete
as last night, or any night before: *not a thing*

is lost. The frail headlights drift, as white as snow
it's fair to say. I'll leave here soon, for good. I know
"for good" is for the better, in some ways, and know
I'll be ready to leave. Or nearly so.

BIRCHES

Generously overgrown,
it's still a kind of clearing:
the sunlight's different here
above the fern bed, somehow
brighter and gentler at once
as birches draw the presence
of clouds down into the forest.

While in this light they suggest
(the narrow limbs, and fair skin
peeling as if with sunburn)
something young and feminine,
they will on an afternoon
black with storm evoke that soon-
to-thunder first stroke of lightning.

In composing complements
to the stolid pine, the sun-
siphoning birches vary
not merely with the seasons
but with the minute hourly
unravelings of the day,
freshly hopeful at dawn in their

tattered but immaculate
bandages and at dusk war-
painted, trunks smeared a savage
red; they are becomingly
multiform and a forest
that boasts even a modest
stand of birch maintains its daily

log of weather conditions
and a hinted timelessness—
as when, given the right light,
birches from their swampy pool
of ferns lift tall saurian
necks to browse, small heads unseen,
in the overhanging leafage.

ALONG LAKE MICHIGAN

The road abruptly changed to dirt,
Thinned until grasses brushed
The car on both sides, and then
Ended in a loop before the marsh.
We hiked along an arm of land held
Firm by cedars, the lake breaking
Like an ocean on one side,
The rippling, flooded wetlands wide
As a lake on the other.
You found a broad white feather
That could perhaps have been
Converted into a serviceable pen;
We searched for precious stones.
Ahead, brown and white shorebirds,
Probably sandpipers, fled from us
Calling with small chipped voices;
So quick, their matchstick legs
Blurred, like hummingbird wings;
And when they finally stopped,
Their low bodies faded wholly
Into the brown and white rocks.
Later, where the cedars clung
Tight against the lake and crowded out
Our path, we turned toward the marsh,
And some rummaging ducks
Scooted raucously away from us,
Wings striking water repeatedly—
Like a stone sent skipping across—
Before they broke with sudden grace
Into the air. We could hear
Waves falling as we wandered
Through woods that held no breeze,
To a small, harsh clearing where

Three or four fallen trees
Crossed in a tangle. We paused there,
In the sun, and something scary slid
As if across the surface of my eye:
Snakes! Among the logs, we began
To pick them out: fat overlapping coils
Lolling in the light, skin
The color of sticks; they were hard
To detect, except when in movement.

Along the lake, where a path had slowly
Collapsed the few feet down
To the shore, up-ending little trees until
Their branches tilted into the water,
We found the body of a doe.
The place was quiet, a pond-sized cove
Where the low waves broke slowly,
Lapping up against the body.
Sand had slipped around the legs,
Blanketing the hard hooves,
But trunk and face lay bare, soft,
The tongue limp and gray beneath
Tiny crooked teeth. A wet eyelash, left
Over an eye picked clean to the bone,
Seemed a tawdry, artificial touch.
I looked for bullets, but found no holes,
Blood, nothing. The massive body lay
Fetid and undisturbed, like a mariner's
Daydream beached up in a storm:
A strange tawny sea-creature . . .
I fanned away the flies that speckled
The blond flank, and we saw them hover,
Land, and then resume their tracking.
We held hands, kneeling beside the body
As if we could impart a gift
Of movement: possible here, on a day
When we'd seen sticks slither

And stones take flight, for this
Animal to rise at our whispering and shake
Sleep from its sandy coat. We watched
The clear waves curl, then break
Against the chest like a heartbeat.

OLD HAT

It was like you, so considerate a man,
to have your papers in order, to leave
your belongings neat; while compelled to grieve,
we were spared the hard, niggling tasks that can
clutter and spoil grief. Yet not even you
understood how a mere cap on its hook,
companion on those outings you still took,
would hang so heavily now for those who,

like you, would keep a tidy house. We've tried
to sort your things, but where are we to hide
those in which some living threads remain?
What we want is to store such things outside
the slow, spiraling loss of love and pain
that turns you, day by day, into a stranger.

THE GHOST OF A GHOST

I

The pleasures I took from life
were simple things—to play catch
in the evenings with my son,
or tease my daughter (whom I addressed
as Princess Pea), or to watch
television, curled on the floor.
Sometimes I liked to drink too much,
but not too often. Perhaps best
of all was the delight I found
waking to a drowse at one
or two at night and my wife
huffing (soft, not quite a snore)
beside me, a comforting sound.

We had our problems of course,
Emily and I, occasions when
things got out of hand. —Once she threw
a juice glass at me that broke
on the wall (that night I drew
a face there, a clownish man
catching it square on the nose,
and Emily laughed till she cried).
It's true I threatened divorce
a few times (she did too), but those
were ploys, harmless because love ran
through every word we spoke—
and then, an accident, I died.

II

Afterwards, my kids began
having nightmares—when they slept
at all; Emily moved in a haze,
looking older, ruined now, and wept
often and without warning.
The rooms had changed, become mere
photographs in which my face
was oddly missing . . . That first year
without me: summer twilight, and those
long leaf-raking Saturdays
without me, and Christmas morning—
the following August a new man,
a stranger, moved in and took my place.

You could scarcely start to comprehend
how queer it is, to have your touch
go unfelt, your cries unheard
by your family. Princess!—I called—
Don't let that stranger take your hand!
And—*Em, dear, love, he has no right
to you.*
          Where did they think I'd gone?
who walked the house all day, all night,
all night. It was far too much
for anyone to endure, and,
hammered by grief one ugly dawn,
I broke. I am still here!—I bawled
from the den—Still here! And no one stirred.

But in time I learned a vicious trick,
a way of gently positing
a breath upon a person's neck
to send an icy run of fear
scampering up the spine—anything,
anything to show them who was near!
. . . Anything, but only to retrieve

some sense that nothing is more
lasting than the love built week by week
for years; I had to believe
again that these were people I'd
give everything, even a life, for.
Then—a second time, and slow—I died.

III

Now I am a shadow of my
former shadow. Seepage of a kind
sets in. Settled concentrations thin.
Amenably—like the smile become
a pond, the pond a mud-lined
bed, from which stems push, pry
and hoist aloft seed-pods that
crack into a sort of grin—
things come almost but not quite
full circle; within the slow
tide of years, water dilutes to light,
light to a distant, eddying hum . . .
In another time, long ago,

I longed for a time when I'd
still felt near enough to recall
the downy scrape of a peach skin
on my tongue, the smell of the sea,
the pull of something resinous.
By turns, I have grown other-wise.
I move with a drift, a drowse that roams
not toward sleep but a clarity
of broadened linkages; it's in
a state wholly too gratified
and patient to be called eagerness
that I submit to a course which homes
outward, and misses nothing at all.

ANGEL

There between the riverbank
and half-submerged tree trunk
it's a kind of alleyway
inviting loiterers—
    in this case, water striders.

Their legs, twice body-length, dent
the surface, but why they don't
sink is a transparent riddle:
the springs of their trampoline
    are nowhere to be seen.

Inches and yet far below, thin
as compass needles, almost, min-
nows flicker through the sun's
tattered netting, circling past
    each other as if lost.

Enter an angel, in
the form of a dragon-
fly, an apparition whose
coloring, were it not real,
    would scarcely be possible:

see him, like a sparkler,
tossing lights upon the water,
surplus greens, reds, milky
blues, and violets blended
    with ebony. Suspended

like a conductor's baton,
he hovers, then goes the one
way no minnow points: straight
up, into that vast solution
    of which he's a concentrate.

Cats of the Temple

TWO SUSPENSIONS AGAINST A
BLACKTOP BACKDROP

Straight up noon, I watch a toad
—dusty, huge—cross a blacktop road
by hops and halts; landing each
time like a splattered
egg, he regathers, heavily pauses
in the baking sun, and heaves
aloft again, again until he makes
the road's shoulder, come
to rest finally under some
dusty asparagus leaves.

Next—and from nowhere,
from right out of the air—
quick as thought
drops a damselfly,
the wings that keep
her motionless an icy blur
of motion. . . . Each at each appeared
to peer: he maybe held
by the sun-enameled
emerald stickpin of her

sparse torso; she,
    by a stolidity
so extreme it looks
    accomplished, a dumb but deep-
rooted contentment. Perhaps,
    of course, this choice encounter
wasn't one and their gazes
    never met; yet they seemed to,
        at least for a few
suspensive seconds that were—

were, obscurely, reminiscent of
    a web I'd found just above
my head that same summer, which,
    metaphor for memory
turned selfless, by a trick
    of the light had altogether
vanished, yielding to the eye
    but what incidence had blown there:
        some seeds, needles, threadbare
leaves, a curled gray feather—

were, surely, irresistible grist
    for the fabulist,
who might well conclude
    that each, true to the instant's
instance, as it urged the
    resolution of mind and mass,
had felt the other's opposed
    appeals, and however much
        could pass between two such
contrary creatures indeed did pass.

THE BURIED GRAVES

From the pier, at dusk, the dim
  Billowing arms of kelp
Seem the tops of trees, as though
    Not long ago
A summer wood stood here, before a dam
  Was built, a valley flooded.

Such a forest would release
  Its color only slowly,
And the leafy branches sway, as they'd
    More lightly swayed
Under a less distant sun and far less
  Even weather. Now, deeper down,

Those glimmers of coral might
  Be the lots of some hard-luck
Town, or—depositing on the dead
    A second bed—
A submerged cemetery. . . . To this mute,
  Envisioned, birdless wood would

Come a kind of autumn, a tame
  Sea-season, with foliage tumbling
Through a weighty, trancelike fall;
    And come, as well,
Soon in the emptying fullness of time,
  A mild but an endless winter.

AN ACTOR PLAYS A TRUMPET

What comes through
in this rooftop conclusion to an old movie
in which somebody who
clearly doesn't know how to play it
picks up a banged-up trumpet
to play against a light-hung screen
meant to represent
a metropolitan skyline

is some sense
of the soaring and transformative strength
of jazz. When he plants
his bandaged shoes, cocks his boyish profile
and lifts the horn to ride a gorgeous roll
of dubbed spontaneity, the effect is (despite
that bogus clothesline at
his back, with its one limp sheet)

persuasive:
those high, ramping notes speak of daring,
the flutter-throated vibrato of
diffidence, and the whole of unformed
invention, wound yet in the horn's warmed-
up cerebric densities. Indeed, so fine
is the music, even his
acting's better for it and as the camera tracks in

on the sure
kiss at the tiny mouthpiece, you might
        almost believe that here
is a man whose upper lip burns, night
after night, in the effort
        to make unpremeditation look
                easy. Although he's
        turning his back on the city, the music

                is a gift
to its boxed-in inhabitants: the loose,
        looping melodies waft
over the roof's edge, falling,
and, in falling, joining
        that collected world of objects you've watched
                falling on film—all
        the briefcases and rifles and bottles pitched

                from tower
and cliff-top, the beribboned packets
        of love-letters lofted over
the rails of ocean liners, the open buckets
of paint, the key rings and miner's flashlights,
        the flying anvils and leather-upholstered
                convertibles and sun
        hats and muddied sacks of gold. . . . Gold

as the moon
ought to be, the pounded streets, the lumpen
heart that weights a man,
stooping his shoulders—just that fleeting,
flyaway color are the tones tonight lighting
off his horn. And when a slow
coldness blows in, a gold-
to-blue harmonic shift, oh

he's dying
up there with the fit sweetness of it,
digging hard, as with a shovel, going
deep for the ultimate, most intimate
strain in his chest. The multi-storied, tight-
plotted metropolis at his feet,
coruscating all the more
for the yearnings he lays upon it,

would topple
if he hurled his trumpet at it.

RABBITS: A VALENTINE

Deliberate
on the rabbit,
who if what you
hear is half true
has found the way
to inhabit
a world without
elaborate
courtship, yet one
flushed with piquant
concupiscent
satisfaction,
a world whose slack
meadowed moments
sit suspended
between frequent
bouts of rabid
raptured action . . .
males of splendid
near-heroic
virility,
females of a
commensurate,
magnificent
fertility.

Ponder this shy
but quite able
go-get-'er, for
whom even sex
is not complex,
who meets and mates,
and keeps no count
but sees the flesh-
of-his-flesh both
diversify
and multiply;
who does not tire
for long, and with
the great outdoors
as his table
banquets on fresh
greens as he waits
for the desire
to mount to mount.

Consider this
suitor of sorts
who advocates
a direct style,
who's sharp on fun-
damentals and
in a twinkling,
his little heart
kicking, is hard
at it; who gets
and forgets while
composing no
explanations,
damnations, grand
pleadings or vows—
disengages
and instantly
begins to browse,
lifting to all
eyes his eyes (oh,
those lovable
black bunny eyes!)
innocent and
intelligent.

IN A BONSAI NURSERY

Nearly nothing
in Nature so
spirits the eye
off—but off by
way of in—to
unveil detail
as minimal
as it's recep-
tive to as does
this more than true-

to-life, living
family of
diminutive
replicas of
themselves, whose pin-
point blossomings
and punctual
leaf-losses, whose
every nubbled
knob and fissure,

knot-imploded
distension and
deep, thematic
torsion reproach
our recognized
but unrenounced
confusion of
size with grandeur.

These pondered, hand-
won triumphs of
containment, come,
tentatively,
of earth-toughened
fingers, father
to son, and on
to son, so long
as the branches
hold on each side,

bid us enter-
tain notions of
days whose hours are
shorter than ours
(shrunken, misted,
mossed-in seasons,
amassed in hard-
pressed heartwood rings) . . .
and enter, please,
a forest where

sun, planets, stars,
and our little
still-swollen moon
are brought, though yet
unreachable,
nearer the roofs
of the trim, smoke-
puffing houses.

A STUFFED TORTOISE

Inwardly re-outfitted over a century ago
according to the handwritten, yellow
three-by-five directly below
the lunging neck, he is, among this petrified
    menagerie, just as once in life,

the oldest of animals. The armadillo
beside him, the Manx cat, the dartlike row
of birds along the wall, all look as though
they never were alive, but whoever re-posed
    our tortoise attended to that

tension which makes him—with the frog and fox—so
didactically adaptable: Who can resist the slow-
paced, cumulative humor of this low-
profiled plodder, who somehow sweeps
    the big races, speaks volumes by example only,

and, fetchingly shy, zeroes inward at any show
of attention—and yet whose narrow,
near-panicky glance is that of some desperado
on the lam? The neck strains, *forward,*
    as if that tough, undersized head

yearned to outstrip its ponderous cargo.
—The time's not ripe for that? If so, the true
burden on his back may be years which offer no
movement casual or quick enough to escape
    a painstaking, on-the-spot review.

POST-COITUM TRISTESSE:
A SONNET

Why
do
you
sigh,
roar,
fall,
all
for
some
hum-
drum
come
—mm?
Hm . . .

A NOISY SLEEPER

I. 1958

The noisy sleeper
in the other room is my
Grandfather whose snores go up & down
up & down like a zipper. Deeper

deeper for the dark
his big breathing climbs
& slips away
like the moon like the day

like Cinny who I so
much wanted to stay
here with me in a bed too big
for me. But Cinny when I let her go

was gone
on her clicking toes
in blackness with the thin slits
open on her black nose

and not a shiver in her chest
for what out there just might
be waiting. She lies at ease I know
on a floor in the night

body curled completely
in the safety of a ring
in whose fur center her head
fits neatly.

In his desk for luck he keeps
an Indian head
penny with the date
he was born which is 1898.

He promised he will look
for one for luck for me
which is 1953.
Whatever

could be that's wrong
what is needed I know
is to be watchful to be strong
simply

though such breathing's far
too big for this house in which
he & I together are
sleeping and I do not sleep.

II. 1983

Recalling now
From the subsiding brink
Of earliest memory
The night-sounds of that man,
My grandfather, is to see
How even at age five one can
Accept reassurances as though
They were believable while
Darkly continuing to think
Things over—to see how
Soon the mind learns to reconcile
Itself to a complex ignorance,
As one begins to know

One does not know.
Now whatever that unnamed
Crisis actually was which placed me
In that giant's bed that night
(Illness in the family?
Some remote, unheard-of fight?
Or, likelier, a disaster lifted
From the blaze of a small boy's inflamed
Imagination . . .) it passed
Much as night passes into dawn,
Unobserved and at last,
Leaving no trace as it drifted
Wholly out of mind. Gone—

Like the existence
Of all others in that house. No doubt
My grandmother was there, too,
Sleeping or, like me, pretending
To sleep, but I don't recall
Her presence, or anyone who
Played with me that day, or what fell out
The next. No, in memory
It's simply two people all
Alone, my grandfather and me,
Bound across the distance
Of a night that rises
And falls and has no ending.

But given all
Memory's shortcomings, one still must
Marvel at its power to restore
The feel of that small boy's fears,
Or the way it can take an old man
Dead now some twenty years
And hold him up close enough
To overhear the rise and fall
Of his slow breathing, just
As though his were once more
The sort of sleep from which—broken
By ruminative snorts, gruff
Assentive gasps—he could be woken.

FLOATING LIGHT IN TOKYO

Having lost track of the time in your own
country, how long you've been up, how little
you slept on the plane, but finding yourself alone
in a small room in an enormous city

you take the elevator down to the dim
lobby and feeling just like a criminal slip
out for a walk beside the moated rim
of the Imperial Palace. It's late—

even the packed, desperate thoroughfares
of Central Tokyo are all but deserted.
Vistas have opened up, and the air's
cooled a bit at last. You can hear

a few horns honking in the distance,
also a heavy truck which, meeting
strong internal resistance,
manfully strains and strains as it climbs

into gear and rumbles off. Such sounds
deepen rather than deplete the sensation
of an enchanted spell of sleep that extends
over miles and millions. Yet it's you

who's about to awaken, as a bend in the moat
reveals a vision—enchanted, too—
of frenzy: a jeweled inner city afloat
in light, the mad neon dazzle of the Ginza. . . .

The neon blazes cleanly in the old moat.
Lights on lights are overlaid in repeated
applications which soothe somewhat
a staggered, jet-lagged brain that longs

to rest yet somehow can't; for they fill
the mind as dreams do, these flourishing
ribbons on the ebony flux, the spill
of moons, keys and horns, the many-petaled rose

and amber and azure blooms that flare
and fade, flare and fade in rocking
even rhythms. How pleasing they are!—
these emblems from a Halloween magician's cape,

these colors selected for brightness alone,
recalling jars of fingerpaint on the low shelves
of a primary classroom. With regret, then,
you note an approaching duck, whose wake shivers

all reflections; and it hurts a little
to watch the neat incision being cut, the plush
collapse begin as the first nudging ripple
swings outwards. Yet as the duck, in passing,

transforms into a swan, the shapely *S*
of the neck lit in sudden fluorescent profile,
and familiar designs begin to coalesce
within the moat, which soon again will reflect

composedly, you'll grant that while the static
glaze was restful, welcome is this
queen of birds with the sea-serpentine neck,
who trails behind her such thrilling rubble.

AT GREG'S

Colder than snow

is how it feels, the year's first rain,
falling on a dark afternoon
the last week of January.

The neon signs

downtown already are blinking,
probably, patchily tinting
the hoods of cars, the ample crowns

of umbrellas

afloat on a washed-in clamor
of honks, whistles, shouts; but here,
upstairs in an old wooden house

five miles away

on the abrupt edge of Kyoto's eastern
line of hills, the darkness and the rain
alike come peacefully down.

It's an old house

that seems older as the rain falls,
rooting out from the walls
a resin whose power it is

to dim all signs—

the strings of dental floss, books
and sweatpants, empty donut box,
stubby pot-bellied hash pipe,

maps and wayworn

backpack—of the current
American tenant,
as if to restore this room to those

whose once it was. . . .

This salvaging illusion (that it's
only time which separates
past from present, and the links still there

by which we might,

stooping, enter yet-simpler houses in
this old capital city, old even then,
of a castled nation whose moat

was the salt sea

itself) is unshaken
by the click-clatter, as of wooden
shoes, of a tall schoolgirl, scooting

along, holding

an opened magazine over her hair,
or by sounds of a distant car,
groaning, as any horse would,

at the steepness

of the hill. The city's
fading, or falling, or folding inwards as,
moonlessly, the cold outspreads itself;

those streams running

freely in the streets will be locked
in ice tonight. It's difficult
not to view this weather

as anything

other than a deepening
tightening, a fiercer colder gripping
of the ground by winter. . . . Only if

you close your eyes

as though about to sleep,
or in truth to sleep,
will the new year's first rain

perhaps summon

that long-gone and looked-for season
for which so many subterranean
spring-wound clocks are set; probably

only to those,

if any, at the shivering limit
of consciousness is it
evident how a colossal, exquisite

mathematical

accounting even now's in preparation,
a one-to-one correlation
whereby each raindrop's knocking shall

have its answer—

together when, then, under
some newly exploded sun, each tight blossom
opens like a door.

IN MINAKO WADA'S HOUSE

In old Minako Wada's house
Everything has its place,
And mostly out of sight:
    Bedding folded away
    All day, brought down
    From the shelf at night,

    Tea things underneath
Low tea table and tablecloth—
And sliding screen doors,
    Landscape-painted, that hide
    Her clothes inside a wash
    Of mountains. Here, the floors

    Are a clean-fitting mosaic,
Mats of a texture like
A broom's; and in a niche
    In the tearoom wall
    Is a shrine to all of her
    Ancestors, before which

    She sets each day
A doll-sized cup of tea,
A doll-sized bowl of rice.
    She keeps a glass jar
    Of crickets that are fed fish
    Shavings, an eggplant slice,

And whose hushed chorus,
Like the drowsy toss
Of a baby's rattle, moves in
     On so tranquil a song
   It's soon no longer heard.
   The walls are thin

In Minako Wada's little house,
Open to every lifting voice
On the street—by day, the cries
     Of the children, at night
   Those excited, sweet,
   Reiterated goodbyes

Of men full of beer who now
Must hurry home. Just to
Wake in the night inside this nest,
     Late, the street asleep (day done,
   Day not yet begun), is what
   Perhaps she loves best.

IN A JAPANESE MOSS GARDEN

After a night of rain
    this garden so
fragile it's never raked, but swept,
    lies on a bed
soft as itself, and all the morning, fed
by the rain banked richly below,
    bathes in a glow

    gentle as candlelight.
    Variety's
ascendant in this lowland where
    a hundred-plus   .
plush samples of the like-velutinous—
star-shaped mosses, amulets, keys,
    bells, snowflakes—ease

    toward freshly minted greens
    which have no one-
word names: rust- or russet-green, pump-
    kin-tangerine-,
copper- and pewter-, frost- and fire-green. . . .
No land was ever overrun
    more mildly, none

yielded with more repose:
    an intertwined,
inclusive, inch-by-inch advance
    built this retreat
where stones are put to rest beneath a sheet
of nap, where limbs are under-lined,
    and where the mind

    meets not tranquility
      merely, but some
dim image of itself—the rounded
    mounds, the seams dense
with smaller seams, the knit, knobbed filaments
all suggesting the cranium,
    as witnessed from

    within. But now this web
      of imagery
bends with a newcomer the colors
    of an unripe
tomato who, beast of another stripe,
untended and rootlessly free,
    apparently,

runs, runs, runs without rest.
        His body gleams
with those pellucid lusters found
        within a night's
last vistas, when a dyeing dawn alights
upon your lids, flooding your dreams,
        until it seems

        your inborn sights and pigments
                outshine the day;
it's morning in a Japanese
        moss garden and
a creature blazing like a firebrand
now makes its episodic way
        between a gray

        stand of toadstools that lean
                like headstones, through
a swampy heel-print, up a fallen
        leaf (and then back
down when it proves an airy cul-de-sac),
across a root, a stump, a dew-
        drenched avenue

of shorter moss that looks
   and feels like felt. . . .
Inanimate, the garden may
      better have met
the thoughtful ends on which its lines are set,
but if its motionlessness must
      come to a halt,

   what cause more fitting than
      this zigzag creature,
bizarre as anything in Nature,
      whose home's a firma-
mental network, a plane of lifelines pitched
upon a random set of reference
      points, a maze which in its

   closed-in stringiness makes
      a self-portrait?
One might view him as captive, too,
      like any prey
inside his web, yet still take heart at the way
he runs to the task, as if to say,
      Today's the very

   day for weaving finally
      a tapestry
at once harmonious and true.

A FLIGHT FROM OSAKA

Into the translucent, smudged, omnivorous wheel
    That the propeller's become
Now slides, block on block and brightly unreal,
    The highflung reaches of sun-dazed Kobe,
        On whose big bay

On this early-summer Sunday afternoon some
    Playfully downscaled freighters
Are lugging broad, ballooning wakes in from
    And out to sea. . . . Quite a leisurely scene
        (Or so when seen

From a few miles up), with one neat, upending touch
    Of real loveliness: the way
Those wakes suggest jet streams—only so much
    Slower to gather, to shatter, to wear
        Themselves out where

Each least impulse is translated into a dense,
    Earthbound medium. The weight,
The piled resistance of those depths, presents
    Us with another, plainer image: one
        Of a hard-won

And never finished struggle with a stone- and vine-
    Strewn soil, a primitive plow
Scratching out, foot by foot, its thin lifeline—
    Into which our buried forebears scattered seeds.
        The past recedes

Much as the circling world does from the round
      Windows of a plane, expanding
As it dwindles into the background, turning
      Both more mysterious and more finely
      Drawn, finally.

SEASIDE GREETINGS

(Oki Islands, Japan Sea)

Together waking to the smell
of new mats beneath us, we find our clothes,
quickly dress, and in slippers shuffle
    down the dark hall

to the entryway, where we trade
slippers for shoes, slide the front
door free, and steal outside
    without a sound.

Our fishing village has not woken
much before us; day is in the splendid,
splashy process of breaking
    over an open

sea and over flooded ricefields
become lavender mirrors, snugly
secured by little green studs.
    We have big pads

of paper bundled under our arms—off
to sketch Yoroi Iwa,
Armor Rock, the crest of a bluff
    which, just as if

something with endless time to kill
on this outpost island had been
engineering an epochal
    if rather small

joke, not only looks like armor but in
its boxy, braided lines is closer
to the Japanese style than
        the European.

    Of course given the scale Nature has
to work with, all of these uncanny,
and often funny, resemblances
        (the ancient trees

    wrung like buxom women, whales
in the clouds, bights like laughing
horses' heads, potatoes bearing profiles
        of generals

    dead now for centuries) are
statistical certainties, nothing
more, and yet they do appease our
        appetite for

    play at the stone heart of things—
a loose, elusive spirit not
about to shimmer its mica wings
        in our smudged drawings.

    Under a midday sun we climb
a treeless, grasshopper-ridden hill
whose summit drops headlong as doom
        to the torn rim

    of the sea a hundred yards or so
below. Hawks ride in the updrafts
and test us with unnervingly
        low, virtuoso

swoops and passes, so near we can discern
how the jumpy eyes pivot in their heads.
Their motions have no waste—glide and turn
  as though they're borne

  upon a refined physics,
an applied mathematics streamlining
toward the pure. We watch their slow arcs
  and plunging strikes,

  cheered to see them flutter
up with empty claws; while nothing we've
ever seen goes about the search for
  a meal with more

  inspiriting grace, our sympathies
are with the homely, camouflage-
seeking mouse, rather than with these
  ferocious beauties.

  . . . Dusk is something taking place
at unreachable distances,
moving off at one remove from us,
  who raptly focus,

  with the fixity of the deservedly
ravenous, on the feast being set
before us—rice, squash, spinach in soy
  and sesame,

sweet ribbons of squid strewn
with pinhead-sized pink fish eggs, pickles,
a sea-bream sliced for sashimi and then
        fitted back in

    around the bones to restore
its swimming shape, a clear soup, bamboo
shoots, lotus root, and two half-liter
        bottles of beer.

    Loaned kimono-like robes hold in
the heat from our baths as we eat,
and as we retire to an embracing
        sudden exhaustion

    larger than we are. Within
each other's arms we lie, neatly, indeed
almost palindromically, placed: settling
        in in an inn. . . .

    The phrase, nearly perfect, is perfect for
tomorrow's postcards, those shiny seaviews
for our friends that might begin, "Dear _____,
        It's lovely here."

ON A SEASIDE MOUNTAIN

(Oki Islands, Japan Sea)

Earlier, as if to conform
to our distant notions of what a remote
Japanese island ought to look like, a warm
sea-mist sifted in, transmuting browns and greens

into the hovering, washed-out grays
of one of those old vertical landscapes
whose ascent to the temple threads a double maze
of fog and foliage. Yet as we climb

from the coast, slips of color filter through—
a red swatch of earth, freshly torn, a green red-
berried bush, green-gold clumps of bamboo—
and the waves' gentle papery crash drifts out

of hearing. To know that the Japanese
seven and again six hundred years ago
banished powerful emperors to these
very islands enriches the mist; far as such

kingdoms are, they'll never be nearer
than while the ground's unreally webbed with fog,
like this, and the air's a breathed-on mirror.
The hills hold, visibly, a second tale,

one—small-plotted, cyclical—of buried toil:
the scaling eye still traces terraces
where rice was grown by hand, and by the handful.
    Ahead, a fall of sunlight, washing some

of the mist from the air, unveils a crust
of prisms on a big rock outcrop. The cloud
cover's coming brightly undone at last.
It's rainbow weather. The bands are there, just

waiting for the right touch of sun.
Yet as we round another bend, the sight we're
treated to is something else again:
a horse, a chunky tan palomino

with milky mane and a calm, discerning
fix to the eyes. The creature stamps, as if
commanding us to halt, which we do, returning
its gauging stare. It expels a long, low

importunate snuffle; then, as if it wants
to make itself perfectly clear, repeats
this sound and, ears up, waits on our response.
None forthcoming, it rears its head, utters a keen

unnerving squeal that seems to hold a bit
of laughter, plunges around (admitting
a glimpse of bobbing genitals, as this *it*
becomes a *he*) and clatters off. . . . He doesn't

go far. A short ways up the mountainside
he stops for us—until we near. Again he's
gone; again he stops. He's become our guide,
apparently. In any case, we follow him

while the remaining mist burns into the sun
until we reach a circular outlook high
above the sea, where nine horses, including one
pony whose mane's so short it stands erect, are

grazing. Head down, duties done, our leader glides
in among his comely fellows, none of whom
show much alarm at having us at their sides.
They huddle closer perhaps, but, snouts in clover,

carry on with the business of the day.
It's so quiet we can hear their surf-like breathing.
    Below, though worn white at the rim of the bay,
the sea by sheer drops precipitately builds

toward an unsounded blue, deeper than the sky's,
richer than mist or history. Whenever
one of these horses lifts its thoughtful eyes
from the turf, stems trailing from its mouth,

this is the view. They eat slowly. The sun's pace
is perfectly theirs, and the planted ease
they are breathing, are breeding, in this place,
while not meant for us, lightens us anyway.

The Mail from Anywhere

THE MAIL FROM ANYWHERE

Mail from pretty much anywhere was nearly
A month in crossing the seas and climbing that island's
Burning hillside. Each day, the heat rose early
And the noon hours called only for a can
Of beer, a cot, and the expunging silence
    Of an electric fan.

The ocean was a blue the sun brought forcibly
To whiteness and the hills a blackened green
Forced white as well. At first you couldn't see
A thing when you groped your way indoors, but soon
Out of the darkness it tumbled, the old scene—
    Chest, table, folding lawn

Chair, hanging calendar, pint-size fridge, sink—
And every stray detail seen to and pieced
Together, including even that runaway blink
Of iridescent green on the backs of the brown
Lizards that prowled the walls. (They were supposed
    To keep the insects down.)

Sunsets were jarring, uncontrolled events,
The monstrously expansive greenery
Revealed at last as veined with blood. But once
The sun was gone, sometimes, a sourceless flush
Would follow, like no other, and the sea,
    Internally awash

With light, turn weightless, while down the beach a masked
Figure might trudge ashore from out a cloud . . .
The air would cool, grow warmly rich with massed
Exploratory scents, and the thoroughfare
Of the Milky Way unroll like an open road,
    As happens only where

All cities lie well under the horizon,
And on such evenings, when the wind was flat,
The bay unruffled, and no moon yet risen,
The heavens would double—stars above, below . . .
That those glints were but the ghosts of fires lit
    Millennia ago,

Such being the time light takes to traverse the sky,
Seems an almost too familiar notion, not
To be doubted—and not to be believed. For try
As we may, and must, the numbers our minds uncover
Will never fit inside our heads. And yet,
    When morning would deliver

Another sort of light—that of a sky-
Blue envelope—here was a gap that could
Be taken in and understood:
            to know,
As the heat-loosened glue gave easily
To your blunt fingers, *A few weeks ago,*
    Someone was thinking of me.

SIGNALLED

Daybreaks to those gray
Voices pushing out
The dark's darker
Voices. And the way

Adoze at times in Kyoto
To the nudgings of a neighbor's
Television and the set
Picking up the radio

My parents always woke to
Morning passing through
Morning on
The other side

Of the wall
Of the world
So early. All
Of those voices

Pushing back
The night as they must
Black into black
The news going on

Out
As it ought
And in coming in
By way of those thin

Pulsed voices saying
On most days Yes it's all right
Everything held together
Through the night

The world is just
Where you left it
Out there you must
Go out in it. Increasingly

The news
Doesn't it
Comes like this
Bodiless

And over blue
Curved reaches the voices clearer
Though farther
Linking us to

Our leaders and voter
Profiles gain
And loss the roaming walls
Of local storms our falling rain

Forests the murmur
Of distant hunger
The murder
Of some public

Dignitary
One of ours and yet
The name not
Caught.

The dead
Pyramid largely
Under us and in their mounting
Numbers would rise

Airing complaints
Apologies second
Thoughts saying Still
Uncorrected

The old mistake
But we're sorry
To wake you we're
Sorry and you must wake.

GLACIER

The sheerly steadied stubborn tons of it

    when you close your eyes
    are something massed
    as a good, pleasing
pressure inside your chest.

The overlapping spill and sinkage of it

    like a wet breeze
    under the wet stars
    works through the dark
revolvings of your ears.

Blindly, you feel it, out there, know you are

    up beside
    an immensity
    that coolly turns
the August sun away.

Or open wide your eyes—they open on

    the mine-black walls
    of the glacier's end,
    hard-fitted with the stones
of its raw erosions. To stand

before what nightless summer cannot melt

    and winter will
    do nothing but
    enlarge upon
surprisingly is not

for you an opportunity so much

    to marvel as,
    with time, to ponder
    how so centerless a coldness
dwindles one's gift for wonder.

Before the outward-locking expulsiveness

    of it, the sharpened
    denial of it,
    you might find helpful
a colossal but simple conceit:

the glacier is a ship; the stones,

    its single freight;
    the sea, its port.
    Home, homeward bound . . .
and casting off from a height

that makes a small, whimsical joke

of whatever gesture—
call or signal—
you'd care to offer
by way of a farewell.

A CANDLE

According to
your point of view,
it stands for love—
or hell posed starkly.
I'm thinking of
the single fellow
who hunches darkly,
as though with shame,
there at the blue-yellow
center of the flame.

REYKJAVIK WINTER COUPLETS

I

One senses
Waking at dark
The promise of dark
For hours yet. The same
Two feet of snow and laval
Outcroppings and a car turning over
Over in search of the position where
    The hum of a dream commences.

II

Disorder's
Undone a few feet
From the bakery door
Where snow-blasting winds
Run up against the firm smell
Of bread baking—loaves white as snow
Within, and shovelled like snow, soon, from
    The oven's blackened borders.

III

The thrashing
And the dead, dumped
From nets to baskets,
Like stolen goods under the old
Warehouse's one bulb gleam. Frantic,
Nearing, the search for them continues:
Hear the wind at the door and the sea, leaving
    No stone unturned, crashing.

IV

As sequel
To a nightcap
Cup of cocoa comes
(Sleep, too, coming on)
The middleman's floating knowledge
That the clouds of steam drifting up
And, out there, the clouds of snow coming down
    Are perfectly equal.

THROUGH TWO WINDOWS

Comforting, in its way, how, wherever you may be,
the effect's so much the same—walking in Rome,

say, or Reykjavik, or one of those rust-red
Missouri rivertowns where we all were born and grew,

you merely glance right up into somebody's home,
catching the sky, out back, through two

sets of windows, and are in a sense home free:
free of everywhere you've lived, everything you've read.

It's a tinted sky—as if by the lives bound like a book
between its panes—and so not quite the one

you're standing under. No wonder, then, these odd un-
sorted feelings of exclusion and remorse . . .

all a small price to pay for any look
at the roof of another world, of course.

A BOWL OF CHINESE FIREWORKS

Late
afternoon light,
and such
a pretty touch—
the way the sun, slow-
wheeling down the wall
in a fall of white on white,
clear into gold explodes
just upon reaching the bowl
of elaborate, illicit fireworks
reserved for this evening's party.

Not
until the night
has grown
into its own
at last, drinks downed,
dinner in all its courses done,
and the guests, trailing bright
inquisitive laughter, led
out onto the black lawn,
will the show start, but already now,
at the sun's touch, it's as if a new

        phase
      has come, a fuse
      begun
      to sizzle. One
by one, the sun picks out
      the big bowl's contents: a long-
tailed dragon first, from whose
gaping leer a leaping tongue
      of particolored flame's to spring;
next, a paisley-papered Roman
candle; then a sort of bouquet,

        bound
      by rubber band,
      of blue-
      and-yellow two-
stage rockets, and a yacht, whose
      maiden voyage (tonight, in a hose-
filled pail) will raise a grand
canopy of stars from the slim pole of its
      smokestack. If, just now, a trace
of pink, of perishable rose, robs some
burnish from the day, as if to say,

        Soon
      this sun-set scene
      must shift,
      its glories drift
off elsewhere—in the meanwhile,
      anyway, our dragon sits in style
atop a glowing treasure-stack,
and with the cool, expansive self-
      possession of his kind,
grins extravagantly back
at the blaze that enriches him.

PLEXAL

Below, on the badly cracked floor
of their heated den, distanced from you by a great
sheet of glass, the pythons (four,
maybe five in all—hard to say for all

the tricky intricacies of their self-made knot)
are sleeping. Though indiscriminately
accommodating (head sunk dreamily in the slot
of another's upflung ribcage, conforming tail warming

still another's tail), they ask to be
counted one by one, tapered end
to end methodically—
a task to which the eye turns

happily, stroking down in gratified leisure
over the charm-inlaid, the bright brute primitive
glamour of their skins. The scales, the larger
of them, anyway, are big as coins,

and metallic, too, in the severe,
exclusionary span of their burnished, brown-
centered spectrum; these creatures come as near
as blooded beings can to seeming

offspring of a blacksmith's lair,
linkages fused under hammers and a bitter sudden
searing kiss of steam.
                    When, where—
all unclear, how the shift begins, but now it's

certain everything's already
moving or must at once be moving; once the long
unclustering's begun, there's not a body
to the whole collective coil

can remain quite as it was: for each,
new, individuating torsions to
work out, new blind ends to reach
within a parted mesh of flexings and dry

oozings. Unclear, as well,
what solidifying hunger or stiffness
pin-prompted the groundswell,
but plainly the correspondences in this den

remain unexpectedly tight—
as with some pared mathematics
wherein the modification, however slight,
of a single postulate inevitably

everts a balance elsewhere, or some ideal
body politic for whom the emergent grievance
of a lone member means the commonweal
itself wants amendment.
                                        Their settling down,

their easeful inching toward one several slumber,
arrives in progressive laxings—
attended, diminishingly, by a number
of afterthought-like adjustments

to show that while at last they've shaped
some workable emplacement, in which to rest
inclusively, they've escaped again
the unwaking repose of perfection.

A NIGHT DIVE

It feels so much
Like waking, this
Rising after
Forty minutes
Under forty
Feet of water;
And to fill your
Life-vest, breath by
Breath, while floating
Nearer a moon
Mounted just high
Enough to have
Lost all trace of
Gold and have turned
A cool silver
Is seemingly
To come at once
Greatly before
The drawing source
Of every blood-
    Tide sleeplessness.

For where, unless
In sleep, have you
Done this before—
Climbing, a lamp
Strapped to your wrist,
Up from the paired
Embers of dim
Crustaceal lives
Fast in polyp-
Padded pockets
At the bottom,
From moray eels,
So much like slow
Flying snakes, from
Schools in flurried
Scatterings and
Voluminous
Fans tenderly
Engorging what
Squiggling minims
    The current brings?

To rise, through rings
On widening
Rings of coded
Compartments-in-
Flux, up to glimpse
Just overhead
The surface where
A kit of bones
Goes dancing like
A skeleton
On a mirror,
And with a crash
To shatter it,
To throw the sea
Clear off your head,
And find the boat
Where it should be,
Nearby and yet
Not yet so near
One cannot feel
   Oneself alone

(Alone within
A sort of field
Where the moon takes
The shivered path
Of a paving
Older by far
Than anything
Pick and shovel
Ever aired) is
To confront, and
As though at last,
The stripped, whited
Ruin written
Into every
Sketchy neural
Blueprint . . . and yet
To confront it
With a moving
Tranquillity,
A long inkling
   That one's fears, too,

Are trifling. *You*
Will come purely
To nothing is
Of course its pain-
Fully unmixed
Message, but who,
Adrift, head moon-
Touched here, could fly
The illusion
That it's enough
Merely to be
A warm, blooded
Body within
So vast a sea?—
Or that other,
By which even
Ever-lightless
Depths are richer
For having some
Mobile mind free-
Floating upon them?

A WORDED WELCOME

Afloat within
an empty sea, and seemingly at home
up there, and floating, too, down here, inside the twin
circles of my binoculars, he ventures quite
without support, since the lifelines
that bond him to that bright
expansive dome

above his head
remain, no matter how I squint and strain,
invisible. Just so: a man's deposited
upon a throne of air, and while he finds it ample,
finds, too, it will not hold him—just.
The resolution's simple:
he must come down,

then. Down through stacked
transparencies, the inward march of far
horizons, he drops—valleys, hills, and meadows cracked
by stationary streams, farms, fences, dots of wool
like waiting building blocks of cloud . . .
No more removable
than the days are

that separate
yearning from some long-planned red-letter day
is each of the one-metre rungs upon that great
notional ladder which attaches him to us;
each outlays its own vista; each is
a sort of terminus
along the way.

Rate, route are set—
the vectored clash of wind and gravitation
fixes the exact details of his arrival. Yet,
from where he loosely stands, views breathlessly would quicken:
blurred trees come crisply into leaf,
a lazing stream awaken
lightly, to motion

throughout a place
whose every glancing form grows sharper-edged—
detail within detail until, with an embrace
whose ardor pops the massive thought-balloon above
his little head, he meets, as pledged,
the rich, soiled earnest of
a peopled world.

THE CRUSH

Harmless, no doubt,
Because hopeless, no doubt, yet far
From hurtless, this nightly not
Being where you are—
Where, somewhere, you go right on being
That miraculously out-
Fitted and not quite conceivably
Tactile matter of yourself. Seeing
How this having you constantly not here
Appears to be my vacant lot
In life, why so implausible, then—that with the mere
Business of breathing, the body's slow
Expulsion of what has turned out to be
    Useless, you'd truly disappear? But no—

    No means, no hope
Of shaking you, though you're not here.
Days, days on end, no end, and so fully aware that I'm
Aware of just how perfectly absurd
It is—how, ever, you pull on me, as though
A magnet to every tiny-toothed gear
And staple, brad and screw, all the drill-
Bits and fishhooks, the hammer claws
And awls, and the metal rope,
Wrenches, vises, planes, rasps, and circular saws
In my belly . . . When, some nights ago, I heard
A summons that withdrew during my climb
Toward wakefulness, until
    I knew it was come from no

Physical phone,
But some dream hook-up, I can't explain just
How desolating that was—only ask you to think
Of a phone ringing to wake the dead in some low-
Ceilinged office whose shades are drawn,
Some Bureau of Incorporations, Inc.,
Some annex of your local Heartfelt Loan,
Ltd., long hours after everyone's gone
Home. No doubt it's some mistake and our
Caller hasn't a prayer of bringing
Anyone to the receiver at this hour,
But still it goes on, that shaded ringing . . .
Still it all goes on, and still, my dear, I must
    Say that I can't say you've brought no

    Pleasure to me—
Pleased, anyhow, at having you enrich
My sense of worlds surrounding ours, in which
(Wouldn't you know?) we are invariably
Lovers. Still, *still no good* . . . No good, you see,
Unless you see, and I don't think you do,
How, daily, you're so painfully untrue
To all those worlds, and what a weight for me
It is, night after night, to field the same
Fatiguingly fresh, petulant demands
For entrance to that room—really not so far—
Where you and I a little shyly are
Undressing and you, yes, whisper my name,
    And I take your head in my hands.

The night of your conception, from the floor
Where we were lying and your mother now
Lay sleeping, I arose. I locked the door,
Lingering there a minute to watch how
The firelight fanned her face and throat, then went
On tiptoe to the misted window, cleared
A space, and found, high over the snow-bent
Forest, a dwindled moon, whose edges bleared
At my slowed breathing—it was all as frail
As that—while far away, or in my mind
Alone perhaps, a dog sent up a wail
That showed him for a wolf. Your mother whined,
As with a dream; a log collapsed; and then
I fingerprinted FIRE upon the pane.

    Dawn, and white lungs, and since it was my turn
To start the fire, I was the first from bed.
Downstairs, where we'd lain watching the logs burn
Gold, red, red to a gray whose core was red,
A killing cold was sliding down the flue.
Yet there it was, cool as the hand of fate:
My FIRE, preserved in hoar-frost, and I knew
She'd love this too.   Well . . . let the (other) fire wait?
Or wake her now? Or—as seemed kindest—make
Of this the day's first story, one that I
Might serve with coffee, last night's apple cake,
And a thawed room? I piled the fireplace high,
And struck a match, wresting a flame, your flame,
From ice. By just such miracles you came.

FIRST BIRTHDAY

You have your one word, which fills you to brimming.
It's what's first to be done on waking,
Often the last at day-dimming:
Lunge out an arm fiercely,
As though your heart were breaking,
Stab a finger at some stray illumination—
Lamp, mirror, distant dinner candle—
And make your piercing identification,

"'ight! 'ight! 'ight!"
Littlest digit, you've got the world by the handle.
Things must open for you, you take on height,
Your sole sound in time reveal itself
As might, too, and flight. And fright.
Some will be gone. But you will come right.

UNCLE GRANT

It was the trip up the Amazon
At the age of twelve that, or so
The boy's mother later insisted,
Undid his wits. How had she ever
Agreed to such a plan? She *had* resisted,
Of course, but the boy's rootless Uncle John,
Writing from a museum faraway
In Washington, and the hell-bent child
Himself, had, between them, won the day
Somehow and made her do what never
She should have done: she let the boy go.
No wonder, what with months in the wild—
Savages, the jungle, food, heat, rain—
He'd caught some fever of the brain.

Whatever the case, this boy, my great-
Uncle Grant, came home to Tennessee
And never left the farm again
For long. Deaths, heat, harvests, he stayed on,
Fished the local Amazon,
Hunted the circling hills. The farm passed
To Alfred, his older brother,
Whose consumptive wife, just twenty-three
And pregnant with her third, miscarried
Ten days before spitting up her last
Life-blood. After a frantic month's wait,
Alfred found his children a new mother—
And, in all, he made his brother ten
Times an uncle. Grant never married.

. . . But the story's more complicated
Than this, since Grant doggedly pursued
An alternate livelihood throughout
His life. At sixteen he sent a kind
Of mash note to his mentor,
Alexander Graham Bell, whose
Avuncular, long, and long-awaited
Reply (from Nova Scotia!) closed—"Choose
Your goals with care, large and small.
Question everything, but never doubt
The resource of the human mind,
My boy." Perhaps it was this call
From Bell, and not the jungle, that skewed
Grant's wits: he became an inventor.

Which was—or was if one can tell
By results alone—the purest folly. His
Dream was of a kind of workbench El
Dorado, where the gold of free
Fancy, mined systematically
At last, would sift itself out.
Not a thing came of his labors
In the end, excepting some
Dubious family tales and—no doubt—
Much laughter for and from the neighbors.
But in the long view—as, say, from
The windows of a plane—bit
By bit his failures feed a soil that is
The richer for those who resisted it . . .

We arrived—my brother and I, each
Competingly agog with the wonder
That boyhood takes in flight—
At the Nashville Airport, there
Met by our tall Aunt Elaine, under
Whose not always watchful eye
We'd spend a month. Next day, we were met by
A list of chores, including some manure
In need of a shovel, which, to be sure,
Was a useful task—if meant to teach
Two city boys never to make light
Of earthbound employment.
                                        Everywhere
Her farm called us with places to explore,
But it wasn't many days before

We'd turned the lock on that old door
And clambered up some stairs to what
Still was called Grant's Laboratory.
It was a low, narrow room, a sort
Of loft above a sort of shed.
Surprisingly, a number of tools
And things still lay outspread
On the cobwebbed table—pulleys, rope, spools
Of wire, bottled powders, a score
Of nuts and bolts, a cracked retort—
The leavings of a mind caught
Up in the perpetual motion
Of the alchemist's lead-fueled notion
Of a lasting conversion to glory.

This was late afternoon. The sun
Again had turned to gold. The room's one
Window gave upon some lilac bushes
On which a dreamer's eye might fall
In those whiled hours when it seems
Unclear if he but dreams or starts to feel
The first buried birth-pushes
Of something real
And richly practical. If Grant's dreams
Were dreams, he breathed no final discontent
In his will, wherein he grandly granted "all
Fruits of my scientific industry,
Now, and in perpetuity,
To the United States Government."

THE CALLER

After the final and all-
But-unnecessary bell, most everyone
Already gone, might come a few last wheeling
Cries, goodbyes, sometimes a brief
Stab of laughter, the last light sliding
Footfalls of this year's children, or
The so much weightier, wider striding
Of one of her colleagues, sweeping the hall
Of its echoes, and then, wider yet, a feeling
Of feeling the building itself being done
For the day—as if it, too, waited for
This moment, and met it with relief.

So she would sit. The room was hers. Late
Afterschool sun climbed the legs
Of the pine desk turned out, years ago,
From the town's own mill. From here: a view
Of Stoner's Hardware, the billiard hall,
And past the tracks, and drearier
Still, the shacklike houses where the town dregs
Lived out their shackled lives, and lastly, below
The town, and also well above it all—
Gray as steel sometimes, sometimes a blue
Earth's freshest eye could but approximate—
The Lake, the only one, her Superior.

So she would sit, and smoke. Her reign here,
In this very room, was now closing upon
Three decades, but always she'd felt bound,
At least until this, her fifty-seventh year,
Never to light up inside it.
Before, she'd shut herself up in what
Was grandly called The Faculty Salon—
That dark and dreary hole. But
No more, no more attempting to hide it . . .
She'd watch the Lake and light up openly—
For anyone and everyone to see—
Had there been, at this hour, someone still around.

Once this same lake was sailed by a giant
Soul, Henry Longfellow, who drifted
On purest tides of inspiration—
This the shining Big-Sea-Water
Of the Arrow Maker's Daughter,
The belov'd of Hiawatha. Oh,
Poetry! On the walls it was Keats, Blake—
Both lamb and tiger—Lanier and Bryant,
And Longfellow over the window, so
The right imagination might be ever lifted
At having read, early on, lines and lake
Together. But where was that imagination?

So she would sit, doubting and smoking freely,
In this her fifty-seventh year. She knew she'd
Scared them all, from the children on up, really:
Parents, teachers—and that squirming sinner
Of a superintendent, too. And she didn't need
Her height to work this on them, though
As for that, proudly six feet tall she stood. No,
This was the fear that those that have no inner
Elevation always feel for those that do.
She knew her poetry. And by God she knew
There wasn't a soul in this sawdust town
Who could, when she felt rightful, stare her down.

(*What a scowl that woman had!* . . . And by
Such phrases, a few thin anecdotes, and one brown
Photograph, this woman, Lucinda Stitt, came down
To me. That's her younger brother, my
Great-uncle Chuck beside her, his cane
The hook to a youthful mishap at the mill.
They lived together. He grins, but she—it's plain—
Distrusts the photographer, whose portrait, cracked
As it is, bears all her rightfulness intact.
She's in her prime, clearly, with some time still
Before cracks of another sort would appear—
In that, her fifty-seventh year.)

What queerish notions, at day's end, brooding
Brings to mind! Sitting, smoking, in a gray-
Golden cloud, she'd wind up recalling
A chant—the boys—so many years ago—and how
Angry it once made her—how angry even now!
. . . She would be newly burning at the way
They had gone on, the boys, including
That jug-eared Gus Gustafsson, bawling
Lucinda, Lucinda, she fell out of the winda.
This was for them the height of wit!
Poetry's paragon! She heard them, chanting it
Stupidly still: *Lucinda, Lucinda* . . .

What was the use of home at night,
His slap of fork and spoon, the lounging phlegm
In his throat, the clearing of that throat
To usher in the utterance of one more gem
Of wisdom? What earthly use? Better to float
Right here, on tides of smoke, still in sight
Of the Lake—gray as steel, blue as flame—
And turn on not one light, but let the room
Go gold, go gray, knowing that of course
He would come, for there was no force
Under heaven to keep him back, come on the same
Cane-clatter, to coax her down from the gloom.

(Well, she was an odd one, that one, Brad,
My grandpa once told me, with a curved
Nudge to the glance maybe meant to suggest,
Man-to-future-man, that she was one who'd had
No use for men. And yet, on a raw,
Rain-paned fall afternoon, Grandma imparted
A counter impression, when she observed,
What a man never seems to realize
Is that even the stoniest-
Looking woman may be broken hearted,
And for the first and only time I saw
A sort of soupy look come into her eyes.)

In winter, ice worked its way outwards from
The shore, outreaching just as if, at last,
About to hazard an actual crossing,
But always followed days of accounting
When, loud as riflefire, it shattered to show
The bright blue burning down below.
No log burned blue as that tossing
Water burned . . . Whyever did it call her so
Fiercely, that blue out of blue, as if some
Answer were wanted she could not give it, no,
It wasn't inside her, no, as the days passed,
Summer coming on, the sun remounting

The legs of her desk, as she waited for the light
To fade, for the ever later dark to come,
For an escape from that man, her clown-
Like caller, looking for all the world like some
Laughably miscast swain in one of the absurd
Town theatricals, mooning out there
On the playground, school being locked up tight,
His round face trained on her upper
Row of windows, baying Come on down,
And scratching his ear, wondering if she'd heard,
Then baying, sweetly, Come down,
Come down, Lucinda, I've made you supper.

Dark would go the walls, rhyme on rhyme,
Now bringing unavoidably to mind
How these were nothing but words in the failing
Glow, one with the down-slipping dust-
Motes, streaks on the glass, red, threadbare
Carpet on the creaking bottom stair
Of home, some other home, and sooner, later,
The Lake must swallow them all, just
As it swallowed, now and then, a skater,
A sailor, whose bodies are flailing
All on the Lakefloor together, blind
As life, as light, as Time;

And colder than ice, somehow, that shattering
Water, and always him coming, clattering
His stick, calling Come down, as if some use
To that, but oh, let him wait, and wait for
The match to bite and the letting loose
Of another ghost of smoke, him calling at the winda,
The window, her name, that man, who won't go 'way,
Shattering the peace, your peace, calling Lucinda,
But he can wait for you, you needn't—no—
Answer, not until you've lit one more
Of the cigarettes that, with each passing day,
Prove harder to light your hands are shaking so.

OLD BACHELOR BROTHER

Here from his prominent but thankfully
uncentral position at the head of the church—
a flanking member of the groom's large party—
he stands and waits to watch the women march

up the wide aisle, just the way they did
at last night's long and leaden-joked rehearsal.
Only this time, it's all changed. There's now a crowd,
of course, and walls of lit stained glass, and Purcell

ringing from the rented organist,
and yet the major difference, the one
that hits his throat as a sort of smoky thirst,
is how, so far away, the church's main

doors are flung back, uncovering a square
of sun that streams into the narthex, so that
the women who materialize there
do so in blinding silhouette,

and these are not the women he has helloed
and kissed, and who have bored, ignored, or teased him,
but girls—whose high, garlanded hair goes haloed
by the noon-light . . . The years have dropped from them.

One by one they're bodied forth, edged with flame,
as new as flame, destined to part the sea
of faces on each side, and approaching him
in all their passionate anonymity.

The Odd Last Thing She Did

A HONEYMOON CONCEPTION
(1952)

All night, though not a flake fell, the snow deepened . . .
From Grand Central their train joggled forth (stray
        snow scraps wadded in gulleys, like
a leafletting not fully swept away)
at dusk; in Connecticut, the darkness opened

(but here and there, a street lamp's sliding glow
showed how the scraps had formed a quilt), as they
        toasted themselves in the dining car,
their glances, given the press of what still lay
before them, sometimes shying toward the window.

In Vermont (though in the sleeping car they kept
the shade drawn and so never saw the play
        of bridal white on white on white,
dark pine fastnesses suddenly giving way
to snow-packed moon-limned stands of birch), they slept,

part of the time. But neither one had ever
been wider awake than on the following day,
        in Quebec, Canada (a city
of foreign signs—*gare, rue, petit déjeuner*—
and everything wrapped in white except the river,

whose fierce black urgings made of the whole place
a kind of high-piled dockyard, every slipway
        loaded with crates of lace and crystal).
On a noon walk, happily mapless, they
chanced a side street and soon came face to face

with a colossal, larger-than-life snowman
in red scarf and blue cape, who, in his warm,
       generous, featureless way, smiled
blessings upon them. (Or snow*woman?*—it was a form
smooth and rich-bellied, as if big with child.)

SET IN STONE

Of legendary littleness,
at least in family circles, was the stone
in Aunt Yvonne's engagement ring. And she knew,
in her arch way, how to expand upon
such smallness: What's this? Why, no less
a natural marvel than her very own
Canardley Diamond. (You
can 'ardly see the thing.) Her needle-point.
Her half-a-glint.

That's all Frank could afford, she would
cry merrily—as poor as that, back then!
. . . Yet a gem of sufficient size to see her through
not only forty years of marriage
but nineteen more of widowhood,
including that last, seated decade when
the vast white shadows threw
a mist on any world that might contain
a thing so fine.

VERY

Something of a surprise
To find her set in black and white,
Although she was, given the portrait's date,
Bound to be. *Red,* I remembered her dress
As *red*—all the more puzzling since
I had so many details right: the out-thrust
Chin (and hip), the healthy bust,
The fervent, faintly cross-eyed glance,
The grand masses of upswept hair,
The hand gracefully but securely placed
Upon the shoulder of the girl in the chair
Beside her, who gazes up with—constancy?
More than that: the humble-faced
Complaisance of the lifelong devotee.

The portrait has a clean-
Angled precision life too seldom shows,
Their branching futures written in their pose:
Clearly, the pigtailed younger one
(My grandmother Cassie) will embrace
As her soul's task the role of the Good Sister,
Who would in every crisis minister
To the other, the Bad One, whose gaze says *Yes,
I'll be there when my ship arrives!*
The Good looks up; the Bad, out and away.
The one is other-, the other self-directed.
What's left them purely is the day-by-day
Embodying of the paired, divergent lives
They have, so early on, elected.

The year's 1916
And the older girl—no girl, she's twenty-three—
Soon will leave Gorvin, Tennessee,
Her home and family, for Washington,
Our nation's capital. She's out to seize
The day, the ring, the prize. The portrait's a farewell.
A *Watch me go.* Or a *Damn-them-all-to-hell.*
Yet who'd deny her her opportunities?
Clearly, she's far too smart, too lovely, too
Lively a blend of fairy-tale princess
And modern girl for Gorvin to possess
Her in the end. Winch up the castle gates.
A bright new roadster's coming through.
Destiny 'phones. Another world awaits.

What awaits presently
Is a William (Billy) Wilmot Morton III,
Whom she will meet the very week she's hired
At the Red Cross dispensary.
Whatever can she hope to set beside
His sheepskin (Princeton) on the wall,
Family (Massachusetts bluebloods all),
And rank (Lieutenant)? What can she provide
Fit for a William Wilmot Morton,
Except her mountain-bred mother wit
And the good looks issuing from
Her too-few decent clothes and that proud name
Of hers—Veronica—which she'll permit
No one (dear Billy least of all) to shorten?

Back home in Gorvin, though,
For that young correspondent who's forever
Posting another homespun letter
An old nickname persists: Cass writes to no
Veronica but "Very." The girl's naive
Presumption that her distant, glamorous
Sister would welcome news of various
Boondock-doings, served up with neither verve
Nor irony (such things as, *Herbert Seaver*
Is building a new barn, or *Jim Duke landed*
A six-pound catfish, or *Old Wally Small*
Does not look well, or *Tripps broke his ankle*),
Turns out, surprisingly, to be well founded.
Who would have guessed that Very was a *saver?*

    She saved, naturally,
Her Billy's billets-doux from France. *They sure*
Do welcome us. Like Sherman said, War
Is swell. And: *As for children? Well, we'll see,*
But I do think four has a nice round sound.
And: *Since I was a boy, reading and rereading*
Prescott, I've always dreamed of heading
to Mexico—I think of it as Magic Ground.
Tlaxcala, Cholula, Chapultepec Hill.
Darling, are you game? They say
It's another world. News of his death (Ors, France;
Crossing a canal; machine gun fire; struck once,
In the right temple) failed to reach her until
Two days after Armistice Day.

She fell less splendidly.
Years passed, about which little's known. There were
To be no trips to "other worlds" for her;
She stayed in Washington. In '23,
Aged thirty-one, she married a Tom Kidd,
Who owned a shoe store. As for children? None—
And no Kidd either, four years on:
Divorce, her first of three. "Her whole life would
Have been so different," Grandma one day said,
"Had Billy lived. *They* were ideally matched.
But when he died—" Her features twitched,
As if she'd pricked herself with one
Of her sewing needles. "—she—she came undone."
"How do you mean?" "Well, she was often sad."

　　　—And often soused, I fear,
For it turned out (my mother later imparted
What her own mother'd been too broken-hearted
To tell me) Very liked a glass of beer,
Wine, bourbon, gin. She had her binges;
At times she was "just fine." In '33
She moved up North, to Rock Ridge, Kentucky,
With husband number four, a Mr. Hodges . . .
Or, you might say, with husband number three-
A, since neither church nor state had ever
Blessed her union with this man—
A triggering irregularity
Turned up by Cassie's husband, Trevor.
And so the Civil War began.

Trevor the autocrat,
Famed for his ramrod posture, knew no doubt:
As far as the family went, Very was *out*.
Henceforth, no dealings—hear? And that was that.
But visits? his wife begged. None. *Letters?* No.
The bond between the sisters was no more . . .
Well, war is hell and Cassie went to war.
She cut off conversation with *him*—oh,
She'd field a question, with a word or phrase,
But that was all. And so it went for days.
She knew, of course, she was outmanned, but mutely
Maintained her ground; it was a sort of siege.
She watched him reason, threaten, redden, rage,
Slam fists upon the table resolutely . . .

The Fall of Trevor Romer
(Still a starred item in the family annals)
Took thirty days. "Along with everything else,
It was for her an endless source of humor,"
My mother explained. "Each time she'd speak of it
She'd laugh till—literally—the tears ran.
He *cursed* her, Poppa, the world's most proper man . . .
What was so dear, though, was just how unfit
He was for cursing women. Well, you see—"
(Now *her* eyes, too, begin to water,
And in my life I've known no laugh so rich
As this, passed on, mother to daughter,
Intact through half a century)
"He called your grandma a real son of a bitch."

But now retreat somewhat . . .
I'm twelve and visiting Grandma and,
Alone in the guest-bed, close at hand,
Seize on a sin that would no doubt
Shock the old girl out of her skin. Mom, too.
And likewise every female of my acquaintance,
Except perhaps . . . And thus begins my dalliance
With *her,* the nether half, the sister who
(Or so suggests her portrait's steamed
Expression, hip thrust tight against her dress)
Might understand my rapturous distress.
(In fact our union's deeper than I'd dreamed:
The strange truth is I soon do dream
Of her . . . Dream that I'm home, my parents' room,

     Yet when I open wide
Their bathroom door, a dark new hall extends.
I walk it *slowly.* Ajar at the end's
A door I open with my knee—inside,
In a hot wash of sun, she's standing. Yes,
Although her back's to me (she's at the window)
There's no mistaking who it is. I *know,*
And when she swings round, in her plush red dress,
Her shoulders are bare and, what's more
In all this heat, they're white as snow. The air's
Ablaze. Her pretty hands are cupped. She peers
At me, declares, *I knew you'd come to me,*
And floats her hands apart. Set free,
Pink petals loop like snowflakes to the floor.)

There was unearthly light
As well—auroral yellows, spacy blues—
On my first night in Vera Cruz.
(I'm twenty-one, it's my first sunset
On foreign soil.) We're eating our way through
A bowl of grapes, at a sidewalk cafe,
Mother and I. "One puzzle piece you may
Not know," she says. "Aunt Very died of—" "Lou
Gehrig's disease." "Yes, which in her case meant
That her coordination slowly went,
Till in the end she couldn't manage locks
And keys, utensils, buttons. It was as if
She was still there but her body'd drifted off."
The spoon in her own hand quakes.

"Before the end she met
A Mr. Stumm, who had a wife . . . (That's just
The start—by all accounts he was a first-
Class bastard.) Big and *mean,* he used to get
In bar-fights and, I gather, sometimes he'd
Hit her—Very—too. Still, he owned a business,
Hardware I think, and paid her bills I guess.
Anyway, though it wasn't contagious, she tried
To keep it from him. The disease.
Afraid he'd leave her. Well!—talk about hell . . .
She should have gone to Momma, but always men
Were who she'd bet on, and now she couldn't tell
Even her lover when the worst blow came down.
D'you see just how un*speak*able it was?"

Not yet, no. Later on,
Though, in my hell-hot hotel room,
I bring her back—the Very of my dream.
Tossing, turning things over, I begin
To gather how it must have been for her.
All the small ruses . . . When he comes
To pay a call, surely she dims
The lights—the better to hide her tremor.
Likewise refrains from picking up
A comb. A plate. A coffee cup.
Get things ready beforehand! Don't
Move much. Stay bright—but what to talk about?
(Each has a job of sorts. His is the rent.
And hers? The same as ever. Putting out.)

I track her to her bed—
Naked, tipsy, the snow of her skin gone sallow,
The once-majestic hair sprawled on her pillow.
The fall of petals has rigidified
To sleet, slamming against the pane.
It's time, and now it's Open wide for him
This body of hers that has become a tomb
Against whose walls he's knocking yet again,
Invoking entry. (Meanwhile, some
Radio romeo's selling songs of love.
Outside, she feels the hick-town streets go numb,
The cold is falling . . .) (Meanwhile, day
By day, the grunted fanfare of
His latest arrival drifts further away.)

1944: PURPLE HEART

"Back—he'd come back, though with a sewed-up chest,
crutches, a leg-cast nearly bigger than

he was, and naturally he's supposed to rest.
Rest? He has to show his girl 'a time,'

out for some splashy meal he can't afford,
and so there we are, he's in uniform and I'm

in a borrowed white silk dress, struggling aboard
a crowded streetcar, and a nice old man

offers up a seat, which, thank you very much,
our soldier accepts—on my behalf. I nearly died.

Sit *in* it? I wanted to crawl *under* it
and not come up, I was so mortified.

I'm eighteen, and healthy—how can I sit
and leave the soldier swaying on his crutch?

★

It was his gallantry is what it was.
Mine would be the first seat had he been well

and was he going to play the slacker just because
one of his knees was peppered with shrapnel?

What could I do? I could have argued across town,
he would never have budged. But when I sat,

the man beside me did—budged—gave up *his* seat.
Only then would our soldier-boy sit down.

It must seem so quaint to you . . . It does to *me,*
and I was there. But things were somehow less—

less absurd, fifty years ago. That's a gallantry
long gone, which is only right"—but not without one

small word of thanks delivered by a son
grateful to have known so choice a foolishness.

What you took away
was something more precious, it turned out,
even than your presence—that of a neat-
knit woman, lined and fine-boned,
    given to lingering at the holiday
        table for hours on end, although
            with little herself to say.

It took us some time—
your death taking us by surprise—
to net our losses. But when questions arose
about some loose scrap of family lore
    (Who was the Austrian martinet
        so strict he wouldn't have his eight-
            year-old son's arm set

when the boy broke it
playing on the banned barn roof? Who
sent the starter's crank winging through
the windshield of his sluggish Model T?
    Who eloped with Phil "the Bill" Hill?
        Who stole his grandma's silver? Whose
            son starved at Andersonville?),

someone would say,
"Edith could have told us that . . ." You
who never married, were never known to
conduct a serious romance, whose
    long career was famously dull
        (linking names to numbers—directory
            assistance for Ma Bell),

and who nowhere seemed
to wring from anyone one single strong
emotion beyond an unthinking
gratitude for your surpassing
   gentleness, managed ultimately,
      nonetheless, to enlist
         and mobilize a multi-

      generational
army . . . now lost, the lot of them, all
of them gone! And they went in loyal
silence, theirs being a campaign
   in which, when history's unlikeliest
      general moved, the troops moved with her:
         on a night-march into the world's least

            understood terrain.

FROM R.E.M.

What made the moment was the lack of all
Premeditation, calculation, talk:
Oh, I was *talking* (what, I can't recall)
Until, look catching look, we slowed our walk,
Stopped still. Right then, now, never having done
Anything on earth like this before, I brought
My face toward yours . . . You had no time for thought.
Instinct alone lifted your mouth to mine.

(The beauty was just this: there was no thinking.
And that I came undone at a mere kiss—
My mind a flood-rush like no flood's before,
Such that no past gasped groping, no headlong sinking
Of flesh in flesh could touch the force of this—
Was a boon, to be sure, but nothing more.)

THE ODD LAST THING SHE DID

A car is idling on the cliff.
Its top is down. Its headlights throw
A faint, bright ghost-shadow glow
On the pale air. On the shore, so far
Below that the waves' push-and-drag
Is dwindled to a hush—a kind
Of oceanic idle—the sea
Among the boulders plays a blind-
Fold game of hide and seek,
Or capture the flag. The flag
Swells and sways. The car
Is empty. A Friday, the first week
Of June. Nineteen fifty-three.

A car's idling on the cliff,
But surely it won't be long before
Somebody stops to investigate
And things begin to happen fast:
Men, troops of men will come,
Arrive with blazing lights, a blast
Of sirens, followed by still more
Men. Though not a soul's in sight,
The peace of the end of the late
Afternoon—the sun down, but enough light
Even so to bathe the heavens from
Horizon to shore in a deep
And delicate blue—will not keep.

Confronted with such an overload
Of questions (most beginning, *Why would she* . . .
So gifted, bright, and only twenty-three),
Attention will come to fix upon
This odd last thing she did: leaving
The car running, the headlights on.
She stopped—it will transpire—to fill
The tank a mere two miles down the road.
(Just sixteen, the kid at the station will
Quote her as saying, "What a pity
You have to work *today*! It's not right . . .
What weather! Goodness, what a night
It'll be!" He'll add: "She sure was pretty.")

Was there a change of plan?
Why the stop for gas? Possibly
She'd not yet made up her mind? Or
Had made it up but not yet settled
On a place? Or could it be she knew
Where she was headed, what she would do—
And wanted to make sure the car ran
For hours afterward? Might the car not be,
Then, a sort of beacon, a lighthouse-
In-reverse, meant to direct one not
Away from but toward the shore
And its broken boulders, there to spot
The bobbing white flag of a blouse?

Her brief note, which will appear
In the local *Leader,* contains a phrase
("She chanted snatches of old lands")
That will muddle the town for three days,
Until a Professor E. H. Wade
Pins it to Ophelia—and reprimands
The police, who, this but goes to show,
Have not the barest knowledge of Shakespeare,
Else would never have misread "lauds"
As "lands." A Detective Gregg Messing
Will answer, tersely, "Afraid
It's not our bailiwick. Missing
Persons, yes; missing poems, no."

(What's truly tragic's never allowed
To stand alone for long, of course.
At each moment there's a crowd
Of clowns pressing in: the booming ass
At every wake who, angling a loud
Necktie in the chip dip,
Airs his problems with intestinal gas,
Or the blow-dried bonehead out to sell
Siding to the grieving mother . . . Well,
Wade sent the *Leader* another *brief word:*
"Decades of service to the Bard now force
Me to amend the girl's little slip.
'Chaunted' not 'chanted' is the preferred . . .")

Yet none of her unshakable entourage
—Pedants, pundits, cops without a clue,
And a yearning young grease monkey—are
Alerted yet. Still the empty car
Idles, idles on the cliff, and night
Isn't falling so much as day
Is floating out to sea . . . Soon, whether
She's found or not, her lights will draw
Moths and tiny dark-winged things that might
Be dirt-clumps, ashes. Come what may,
The night will be lovely, as she foresaw,
The first stars easing through the blue,
Engine and ocean breathing together.

AT AN ISLAND FARM

If only the light might last,
the mild sea-breeze hold steady,
I think perhaps I could soon be ready
to relinquish a past

that let go of *me* as surely
as some stern wind last year
may have seized a wheat stem by the ear
and shaken it, purely

without a thought for
whether the seeds were drowned
or whether, aloft, some few of them found
another shore.

LATER

The goal I suppose is a steadied mind—
to replace with wood and stone
and insulated wire
what was contrived of flesh and bone,
blood and blood's desire;

isn't the final end to find
that haven where where you are
matters as much to me
as whether or not, on another block,
the wind's now ruffling a tree?

RED LEATHER JACKET

Had I not spoken first
when we met that clouded morning
after a broken night
in which we'd slept apart;

had I not stunned myself
at the start I underwent,
kindling at the sight
of you far across the park

(bright—so bright your jacket's
red on that dark day
whose fallen leaves were drifting
from brown to a final gray);

had I then, possessed by a flame
that stirred up the ashes of
a cool cover of pigeons,
not broken into a run

(past a row of frost-gripped benches
and a low, a wire-caught kite
that hung its head in shame),
and reached you almost breathless;

well, suppose I hadn't spoken
first, dipping my head
toward a spooneristic kiss
from you who glowed as red

as any Queen of Hearts,
hadn't cried, "My dear, you luck
like Lady Look herself!"
would *you* have managed better?

What would you have said?

PLUS THE FACT OF YOU

The sun, having come
down hard all day, goes out softly from
our limbs tonight, the burn we'd otherwise
   be feeling tamed to a banked glow
by one of the white, magic lotions pulled
   from your big black sack of supplies.

   We're both up to the brim—
with rice, little shrimp, red snapper aswim
in a spiced lime-laced broth, greens in a mustard
   vinaigrette, black beans with cilantro
and chilis, pineapple wedges, papaya,
   coffee, some nutmeg-dusted custard.

   And my head's brimming too,
for as I'm drifting off, my back to you,
your breathing seems to flutter through a green
   undergrowth and I'm standing where
this morning we stood, dumbstruck to behold
   more flowers than either'd ever seen

   outside a garden: one
whole hillside under blossom, overrun
as by a river, golds, whites, pinks, reds, fluid
   and aflame!
               (But now my sleep-tilted
task is to compute if blooms outnumber breaths,
or breaths blooms . . . And let's say you take

eight breaths a minute, that's some sixty
minutes per flower and don't forget to carry the one but which
one is it?—and why at night do numbers clamor so, packed
    too tight too are they, no other room
to bloom, carry the one?—carry the sun under your skin,
    we do, and if you add a one to two, too? . . .)

    I arrive at my sum
down at the base of the slope, where I come
upon you, slyly deep in foliage,
    sheltering from the sun,
dipping hot red feet in a bouldered stream,
    three buttons of your blouse undone.

SMALL WATERFALL:
A BIRTHDAY POEM

Maybe an engineer,
stumbling on this small, all-
but-forest-swallowed waterfall—
a ten-foot drop at most—
could with some accuracy
say just how much energy
goes unharnessed here.

Enough, is it, to bring light
and heat to the one-room hut one might
build here at its foot—where,
piecing together the *hush*
in the current's *hurl* and *crash,*
a lone man might repair
to fix a shopworn life?

Enough, anyway, to light
one image in my head: this mist-
laced column of water's
as slim as a girl's waist—
yours, say, narrow still despite
the tumble down the birth canal
of a pair of nine-pound daughters.

Well, there's nothing for it but,
sloshing my way across the pool,
I must set whimsy into fact—
which is how, one blazing, cool
August day in New Hampshire, I
come to be standing with my
arms round a cataract.

. . . Nothing new in this, it turns out—
for I know all about embracing
a thing that flows and goes
and stays, self-propelled and -replacing,
which in its roundabout route
carries and throws, carries and throws
off glints at every turn, bringing

all it touches to flower
(witness those flourishing daughters).
    Your reach exceeds my grasp, happily,
for yours is the river's power
to link with liquid, unseen threads
the low, far, moon–moved sea
and the sun's high–lit headwaters.

A FALSE SPRING

(She who'd been taken
hostage—when?—been bound
and drugged, kept in all things
in the dark, now at last found
she'd begun to waken.)

*So gently that year did
January come on, it teased
out the crocus, half-hid
in snow, gilded the willows, eased
the forsythia into bloom.*

(But a good hard blow
sent her blindly back under.
Escape? A mere dream,
and that the dream came in a glow
of green, of gold, no wonder.)

YET NOT YET

Yet what do you answer
the voice within that cries
on the first day of a long-delayed spring,
But it all comes too soon!

Before we are ready for
so heady a prize
a thousand icy streets must be paced
under an iced-over moon.

AFTER THE DETONATION
OF THE MOON

Hate Winter? Here's a Scientist's
Answer: Blow Up the Moon

Headline, *Wall Street Journal*

We *were* overwhelmed, just as they'd intended:
for wasn't this the greatest show of clout
the world had ever seen, and all without
loss of a single life—an exploit splendid
no less for its humanity than for
its sweeping expertise? And they were right
that life would go on as it had. The night
was still the night. The stars blazed all the more
in a cleared sky.
                      These days we seldom fall
for that trick of the eye by which some tall
mist-softened clocktower or fogged street lamp will
recall a changing face, and something tidal
heave in the chest, then ebb, leaving us all
to wonder when if ever this sea too might still.

PLAY

I

Easily, first our red canoe's
upturned reinforced nose

coasts across the rounded rim
of the bridge's shadow, then a room-

like enclosure's thrown over our shoulders and we're
in on a sort of open-ended show, where,

back and forth on the rusted ceiling,
up-angling sunlight's sailing.

    Yet it's a harbor where, try as we might,
    we can't hold our own, quite,

    and though we paddle backwards, hard
    toward the bow, we're spirited off—yard

    by yard, driven irresistibly along,
    back under the sky. The current's too strong.

II

Even so, we're under long enough to bring the scene
lastingly to life: a zone where the sun,

though splintered, crowns another domed firmament,
this one brown, and the river's roofed voices mount

to a ceaseless, clamorous *hush* . . . a place where
spiders in tatters live out a high-wire

existence, somehow coming to base
their very lives above the onrushing abyss.

     Upon the bridge's underside the broken sun, too,
     throws a web, pliant and vast, and through

     the spider-nets the solar-nets brightly go flying,
     as if to show up the uselessness in anyone's trying

     to snare, however fine the line unwound,
     matters of spirit in the matter-bound.

III

—Or are we, in our rush to extract
lessons from the place, almost tricked

into missing the all-but-unmistakable? Might it not
be play, purely, that slides the one net

inside the other—the selfsame urge that bends
monkey tails into question marks, lends the clownfish bands

of motley, builds, of blackness, the more multi-mooned
of our planets and the see-through micropalace of a diamond?

> What but play's at work, when an old bridge (one that must
> groan and shudder each time, in a rolling hill of dust,

> another flatbed truck comes heavily
> rattling over) all the while turns out to be

> undergirded by a mesh of wheeling
> water-filtered sun across its nether ceiling?

AN OLD HUNTER

Up at four
and proud to make no delay; as the car
comes sliding up the drive, headlights dimmed,
he's slipping out the door.

At first he's
a little edgy, seeing they're all—
the other three—some thirty years his junior,
but soon a companionable ease

settles in,
with talk of the Lions (another loss),
a stolen lawnmower, someone's vanished girl,
and a few nips of gin.

It's not long before
he knows they *like* him—listening with clear
interest to his one short, pointed, wary
anecdote about the War.

And all the while
heading North, toward cleaner air, and trees
as if cleaner too—the shadowed oaks
lightening, mile by mile,

into birches bright
as lightning strokes. It looks like rain . . .
And it turns out every tree they pass,
and each small-town traffic light,

barn and billboard
and shaggy, disused railroad track,
all the clipped fields and the tall powerlines
steadily propel him toward

a naked, mud-brown
thicket beside a long low lake,
there to huddle with his rifle, and to wait,
as a fine rain comes down.

Oh, just to shake
the *chill* from his bones—but it's lodged so deep
even the bourbon in his flask can hardly
nudge it—and his knees ache,

and his shoulders ache,
and it's almost as if nothing will happen, ever
again, except the cold rain go on shivering
the dead surface of the lake.

★

So he slogs his way
out through the mud and back to the cabin,
hoping against hope he won't be the first of the group
to have called it a day—

which he is.
To make himself useful, he builds a big
fire that will welcome the others, and so they'll know
this little break of his

was meant to be brief,
he doesn't remove his hat or his coat
before drawing a folding chair up to the blaze.
But what a relief,

Lord knows, to feel
the heat go stealing through his calves!
He lets his eyes close, and though he doesn't sleep,
his glowing lids reveal

room upon room
of ideal gold, walls gold, and floors gold,
and each room warmer than the next, as if
in time he must come to some—

He's not asleep,
but when a log, hissing like a snake,
snaps with a resounding bang, his eyes spring open,
his old hands leap:

for a moment all un-
certain if this blast sent booming,
booming across the lake, comes from his own
or someone else's gun.

BLESSING FOR MALCOLM LOWRY

His was a discriminating taste for error.
He once pinned a sharp little poem
on a printer's lapse—*tavern* appearing for
cavern—and in fact from the cavernous rear
of a bar one night I heard a rounded voice,
ripe with top-heavy certitude, pronounce,
"Life's a process of rile and terror"—
which too no doubt would've appealed to him.

This morning, early, I typed *damn* for *dawn*
and thought of him mumbling home, stumbling, cold,
daybreak, heartbreak, words in the head a flow
too full to follow, vows of a better life somehow
turned bitter: bitter laughter . . . A new leaf? The old
relief—and another damn day done in before the dawn.

SHILOH, 1993

On the cold battlefield
in the mists before sunrise
they run through a series
of feints and forays,
the old pair of adversaries:
blue sky-patches advancing
as the gray shadow-shapes fold
into copse and fence row and back road . . .
It's the oldest tale
in the world: no convincing
some two to call a halt until
their shades of difference disappear
in the uncontainable outpour
of another spill of red.

CREST AND CARPET

I often picture it as a great cold
mountain—your death—as if you

selected it somehow, chose
your treeless summit from which to stare

down on us forever: the world's flat, there
in that vision I hold to, and yet goes

on unrolling beneath you, or being unrolled,
like a carpet, and each day's a new

turning, a further spreading out,
and I wonder of you on your mountain Just

what can it be like, how must
you be feeling, as you watch friends

and family busily go about
their ever more distant errands?

Curves and Angles

CITY ALBUM: A WET AFTERNOON

I. Dorm Room

Theirs is that special condition of plenty
    available only to those with nothing
        on or between them. It's as if they'd been
    out in the downpour, bodies wet as
        that—but they've stayed in all day. Again
    he studies her nape, fingertip-tests her hip.
He thinks her *very young*. Eighteen. He's twenty.

II. Basement Lab

The entomologist drops into a pool of light to peer
    at the magnified maxillae of a rare beetle
        while something lackluster raps the dusty pane
    above her head, a passing fluster of drops
        hardly worth speaking of as rain;
    she bagged this firebrand, *Pyrophorus ignitus,*
on a slope that catches two hundred inches a year.

III. Rectory Study

A working drowse having overtaken him
    in the middle of a chapter, Father
        Ciprielli, who has led the boys,
    his fresh recruits, into Gaul every fall
        for forty years, now shuts his eyes.
    The same grammar that carried him off will,
when it slips from his lap, soon, awaken him.

IV. Halted Train

It's too perfect: can the small boy on the train
  really be an OTTO (as finger-printed
    on the steamed-up window), a name
  not only palindromic but bilaterally
    symmetrical—and therefore the same
  for his two circles of readers, those in the warm
interior, and those reading backward, out in the rain?

LITTLE SCHOOL IN A JUNGLE

(Micronesia)

Summer vacation's come
to a land of perpetual summer.
The windows have no panes—
no need for keeping out the weather
where every wind is warm, though there's a call for these
big overhanging eaves as shelter from
the driving rains.

Wire mesh in place of glass—
windows to expel from school
nothing but the stray
scavenger, human or animal.
The insects' rusty clockwork-cries, the jungle's deep
competing smells—these drift in, out of class,
night and day.

Two models of the world
perch upon the teacher's desk,
although in either case
old Earth's seen better days: a plastic
ball that has lost some air, or else a rigid sphere
whose peeling surface, strip by strip, has curled
into outer space.

(Glue in this climate's quick
to give way: tin cans shuck their labels,
books split along the back,
furniture sunders at the joints;
and at each opened seam, meanwhile, the race is on
to knit things shut again, as mold grows thick
in every crack.)

Whichever world you'd call
your own—the sack slumped on itself,
the flower whose petals fly—
it isn't likely to record
so insignificant an island, notwithstanding
all the brash longing as the rough hills sprawl
against the sky.

What hills the children see
are not found, then, on the classroom globes . . .
and still less the rock slides,
the ten-foot waterfalls, the tight paths
where pigs run, the brown shell of the downed warplane, and
the ever-shifting, unshakable greenery
on all sides

(a tapestry that can
swallow complete an object small
as a schoolchild reared within
a village tucked away within
fold upon fold, foot after foot of towering
jungle on an island no bigger than
the head of a pin).

NOT LUNAR EXACTLY

(Detroit, 1948)

New, and entirely new to the neighborhood . . .
One August day, it came to their own street:
the Nutleys brought home a television!
Nights now, the neighbors began to meet
more often than before, out walking,
walking past the Nutleys, who, on display
behind their picture window, sat frozen
in their chairs, watching their television, which lay
    off to the side, just out of view,
    so you couldn't make out what
    it was they were watching but only
    them watching, the four Nutleys, in a blue
    glow that was lunar but
    not lunar exactly.

That was the summer we all
watched the Nutleys—no,
we all watched *The Nutleys,*
which was the one great show
of the summer, it ran for weeks,
with its four silent stars
behind glass, until nights went cold
and damp and we turned to our cars
    if we ventured out after dark,
    and then—three in a row—
    the Daleys, the Floods, the Markses
    took the plunge, they brought home the glow,
    and the Nutleys, suddenly,
    belonged to a new community.

MIDSUMMER, MIDWEST

We played a game called 4-Square
With a lemon-yellow ball
In the street after dinner.
We kept awaiting a call

From somebody's parent, ordering us in,
But (amazingly) no call came,
The still-bright ball
Went round, we went on with our game—

Voices no doubt lifting
To where the Dawkinses' grandmother lay
Winded by emphysema,
Who hadn't been out all day

And had now minutely to ponder
How this evening's sunset would fall
On the plaster homeland of hummocks and craters
Of the guest-room wall.

SON

Memory buries its own,
And of what now forever must be
The longest day of his life
What mostly remained was a blur
Under too-bright lights—so he
Could scarcely tell if the things
Sharpest in his mind were
Nothing but fantasies, sewn
Afterward, out of grief,
And guilt's imaginings.

Yet it seemed memory called up
(After the interminable birth,
As his finger stroked the arm
Of a child who would not last
Even one whole day
And all of its time on earth
Ministered to by vast
Machines that couldn't mend the harm
In a single transcription slip
In reams of DNA)

A look so haunted, so
Haunting, he would not confess
(Not even later, to his wife)
How it stayed with him, on him: the slow
Flicker in a watery eye,
The mute call—through all
The exhausted hopefulness
The condemned come to know
In the end—from animal to animal,
Imploring, *Please save my life.*

LORENZ

Now and then he would drop from sight,
days at a stretch. No doubt he found his way
    to drink—some suitcase full of spirits—
    and, likely, to some paid romance;
    he knew the poignancy of *that*
from both sides of the street—the dwarfish man
        who wrote "Ten Cents a Dance."

I think of him, his low head low,
trundling through some dim, ratty hotel lobby.
    Under his breath, he curses when
    one of the great ones ("Blue Moon," say,
    or "I Could Write a Book," or "I Wish
I Were in Love Again") again comes piping
        over the p.a.,

    at his side some sweet-faced young man—
or sweet enough—or young enough—who hails
    from those spellbound Great Plains (his story
    a pretty once-upon-a-time)
    where silos grow instead of skyscrapers,
horizons call, and nobody has ever
        heard of a triple rhyme.

This young man isn't apt to know
the melody (the elevator door
    clangs shut, the huffing car ascends),
    and still less, thankfully, the neatly
    turned tortuous lyric. . . . Soon now, a gorgeous
silence will bloom, and the unworthy, wordless at last,
        disclose himself completely.

A GOOD LIST

(Homage to Lorenz Hart)

Some nights, can't sleep, I draw up a list,
    Of everything I've never done wrong.
To look at me now, you might insist
    My list could hardly be long,
But I've stolen no gnomes from my neighbor's yard,
Nor struck his dog, backing out my car.
Never ate my way up and down the Loire
    On a stranger's credit card.

I've never given a cop the slip,
    Stuffed stiffs in a gravel quarry,
Or silenced Cub Scouts on a first camping trip
    With an unspeakable ghost story.
Never lifted a vase from a museum foyer,
Or rifled a Turkish tourist's backpack.
Never cheated at golf. Or slipped out a blackjack
    And flattened a patent lawyer.

I never forged a lottery ticket,
    Took three on a two-for-one pass,
Or, as a child, toasted a cricket
    With a magnifying glass.
I never said "air" to mean "err," or obstructed
Justice, or defrauded a securities firm.
Never mulcted—so far as I understand the term.
    Or unjustly usufructed.

I never swindled a widow of all her stuff
  By means of a false deed and title
Or stood up and shouted, *My God, that's enough!*
  At a nephew's piano recital.
Never practiced arson, even as a prank,
Brightened church-suppers with off-color jokes,
Concocted an archeological hoax—
  Or dumped bleach in a goldfish tank.

Never smoked opium. Or smuggled gold
  Across the Panamanian Isthmus.
Never hauled back and knocked a rival out cold,
  Or missed a family Christmas.
Never borrowed a book I *intended* to keep.
. . . My list, once started, continues to grow,
Which is all for the good, but just goes to show
  It's the good who do not sleep.

A TEENAGE COUPLE

He said, or she said
(Desperate to have their say),
You know, we may not last forever. . . .
And on that unthinkable day

(She said, or he said—
Somebody *needed* to know),
Who will be the last to turn and look
After we've agreed to go

Our separate ways?
(Which one, that is, will be the one
To watch the other hobbling off,
Black against the sun?)

BREAD AND CHEESE

What pulls the cloud together,
some thirty feet below the surface, creating
purely from particolored fish
      a sort of submersible thought balloon, is,
truth to tell, nothing more ethereal
    than a can of Cheez Whiz—

brandished by a diver wearing little
besides an airtank. No strangers
to such come-ons, the fish, chiefly the reef's
      pretty riffraff, are brash and too well fed;
the cheese—or cheez—extrudes into the sea
    as a sturdy gold thread,

which the bullies of various schools
come and snip right off the nozzle
with a satisfied, if inaudible,
      snapping swallow and the smug look
of an old scrapper who again has taken
    the worm without the hook. . . .

And the diver? In his heavenly blue
strip of a swimsuit, he's just the sort of
god you'd imagine, a solar con-
             densation, burly and bare,
all long gold limbs and a restless
    halo of long gold hair—

perfect complement to the good gray
woman parked on a bench (an urban archetype),
gloved on the balmiest spring day,
             who dwells in her own living cloud: such
a fervent crowd of grime-gray pigeons they
    (seeking a soft touch,

and the loaf's soft white innards) nearly
cloud her out, cooing formidably,
as she coos back at them, forbearingly,
             urging *Patience, patience,* though she knows theirs
can be such a hard-hearted town,
    the poor greedy dears.

THE WATERCLOCK
AND THE HOURGLASS

An old pair of parents, it appears,
In an old museum case . . . He unites
Form and function, plainly; she's a thing
Of fancy and flourish, and is—for all her years—
Exceptionally pretty.

He springs from Cathay, land of whispering
Bamboo and gently rain-wrung skies;
She's of Venice, a flowing city
From whose brisk ovens
Glowing loaves of glass rise.

A mixed marriage, then, but by all lights
A happy one (differences reconciled—
They've learned to take things day by day),
Save that their only, problem child
Keeps running away.

A SCIENCE-FICTION WRITER
OF THE FIFTIES

I. When the Smoke Rings Sail

Although it scarcely matters where he is,
He's in Urbana, Illinois, tonight,
As he is on most nights; it's where he lives.
Move to New York, they're always telling him.
Or *San Francisco, L.A., Washington*—
As if these places were appreciably
Nearer, somehow, to what he writes about.
Even his friends, they don't grasp that all places
Are roughly the same distance when your subject
Is Time itself, the pure future. . . .
Besides, he's drawn to these Midwestern skies,
Clean and enormous, stars all the way down
To the horizon, where the very lowest
Float at eye level and the illusion is
You're walking to the stars.
                                        Most nights, he walks:
Studies the sky; hums a bit; smokes his pipe;
Under a streetlamp sometimes jots a note
Into his notepad; mostly, though, just walks,
Letting his mind wander. One night the moon
Called up a boyhood marble, rolling loose
Within the hold of some colossal ship
That might be thought of as a drifting speck
On a sea lit by a colossal moon.
He wrote that down. You never know. . . .
He writes "boys' books"—or so he's sometimes told.
Well, true enough, his plots employ their share
Of rocket ships and anti-gravity
Devices, time-machines and -warps, and creatures
Spawned on far planets.
                                        Boys' books? He won't argue

The term, in any case, except to say,
Who knows? Maybe the kids have got it right.
And maybe growing old is just a way
Of drifting from the truth. In *Astral Children*
He brewed a world where aging is a form
Of madness, and the sane stay young forever.
Whatever his books were, he wrote them fast,
A new one every year, with luck—and yet,
For all his speed, hardly enough to keep him
In pencils, carbon paper, pipe tobacco.
Invasion of the Mantis Men—that's his,
And *Time's Knock; Old Earth's Torn Mantle; The Gears
Of History.* Although they were his children,
He rarely glanced backward; no, *his* way was
The alligator's—lay your clutch of eggs,
Kick some loose sand on top of them, move on.
Perhaps he liked *The Teleminders* best,
The one where scientists learn to project
Human-sized intellects into the brains
Of animals—a bear, a camel, even
Spiders and termites—only to discover
That these emancipated creatures, while
Keen to communicate among themselves,
Still want nothing to do with mankind. . . .
Those typo-riddled books of his—cheap glue,
Cheap stock, cheap artwork—were all paperbacks,
Some housed within a sort of duplex, his own
Book with some total stranger's book attached,
A two-for-one special.
                          Cohabitation
Was not his *forte,* it seemed, though any man
With five ex-wives and seven children surely
Might figure at least *one* would live nearby,
Lending companionship when things turned hard.
Things have turned hard for him. Tonight he walks
Through his adopted hometown of Urbana,
Streets dark, stars bright (it's very late—two, three,
The unwatched hours he always has loved best,

When the mind's gravity loosens a little),
And what's a man to do with such a sky
But launch a couple smoke rings that resemble
Little life-vests (he wrote down that one, too),
For little lives afloat on Time's great waters?

Time is his element, who wrote *The Clock*
Of Ages, Dinosaur Robots, Big Minutes.
Time: it's two weeks now since the diagnosis
Of non-Hodgkins lymphoma—a rare "oma"
Lodged in the lymph system and seemingly
Dead-set on killing him. (By definition,
Of course, what kills you is a rarity:
That one one-in-a-million exit door
That's got your name on it.) Soon, in the blink
Of an eye—Thirty years? Fifty?—they'll find
A cure for this disease; yet he'll be gone
Before that blink occurs. (Which means? His death's
One more accident of timing. . . .)
Yet it turns out to be more difficult
Than he would ever have supposed to square
His personal extinction with the heavens;
It has grown hard to gaze up at the stars.
They agitate him in a way he hasn't
Felt since grade school, back in those blazing mornings
When love—the real McCoy, a hopeless passion
Larger by far than he was—swept him so
Feverishly, his body shook with it.
It seems (wouldn't you know?) he'd fallen for
The class queen, Betsy Wren, and couldn't bear
To look at her, almost, and couldn't bear
To stop looking: bold glances that avowed,
Others are bigger, stronger, even funnier—
And yet, belovèd, I'm your most devoted.
That's just the way the stars now make him feel;
He throws them pleading and assertive glances.
(*I* am the most devoted.)
                         The cold stars?

Their coldness, too, is but an accident
Of timing: yes, their hospitality
Will be revealed in Time, his element,
Which flows unseen across the glittering
Riverbed of the sky. It's all the heaven
He's ever asked of Heaven: to see the stars
For what they are: half-submerged stepping-stones
To zones some unimaginable race
Will homestead when the sun's a guttered candle.

II. *When the Smoke Clears*

The mind, that rambling bear, ransacks the sky
    In search of honey,
Fish, berries, carrion. It minds no laws . . .
As if the heavens were some canvas tent,
    It slashes through the firmament
To prise up the sealed stores with its big paws.

The mind, that sovereign camel, sees the sky
    For what it is:
Each star a grain of sand along the vast
Passage to that oasis where, below
    The pillared palms, the portico
Of fronds, the soul may drink its fill at last.

The mind, that gorgeous spider, webs the sky
    With lines so sheer
They all but vanish, and yet star to star
(Thread by considered thread) slowly entwines
    The universe in its designs—
Un-earthing patterns where no patterns are.

The mind, that termite, seems to shun the sky.
    It burrows down,
Tunneling in upon that moment when,
In Time—its element—will come a day
    The longest-shadowed tower sway,
Unbroken sunlight fall to earth again.

III. After All

Cheap stock, cheap artwork—everything just
So deliciously cheap! They pull on me still,
Those sci-fi novels of the Fifties,
And when in some used bookstore,
On a shelf where old futures gather dust,
I happen on one I knew before,
Years back, I undergo a little thrill

Of dislocation.
           They pulled, originally,
On my father, who housed them in the attic, where
Each startling cover was privately digested
By a boy too young to read: pirate spaceships, and square-
Headed robots with ray guns, and heaving-breasted
Girls lashed in the arms of antennaed aliens . . .
What a queer place the future would be!

The few facts I knew about outer space
Haunted me. On those other planets, the ground
Hides a different gravity. You might float away
Like a balloon. The stars don't twinkle. It's always day,
Up there. And black as night. The dark vacuum
Would suck the air from your face.
If you cried out, there would be no sound.

. . . All those hours in the attic, devoted
To an eager, uneasy analysis
Of the lurid covers on my father's shelves,
Left a lingering hunger, even now unfed—
A yearning for a place the books themselves
Couldn't supply, since (it must be noted)
Most of those books are better left unread.

And yet, now and then over the years,
I've picked one up and read it, particularly those
Of the man found more often than any other
In my dad's ragged collection: the author
Of *Old Earth's Torn Mantle* and *The Gears
Of History* and *Big Minutes* and *Time's Knock,*
Who died one month before the launch of *Sputnik.*

Like most of his contemporaries,
He interests us for what was *not* foreseen,
The upheavals he failed to anticipate:
Book after book of his, the white race reigns
Unchallenged, sex is always straight
(But not straightforward), and women are keen
To fix the meals and be the secretaries.

(Oh, those tart-tongued but true-blue
Gals of the twenty-first and -second centuries,
Dizzy and desirable as ever! You knew exactly
How they're dressed without his telling you:
Blazing red lipstick, thick penciled brows,
Off-the-shoulder blouses, skin-tight capris,
Firm girdles and those pointy Fifties bras.)

226

And yet—of this I feel quite sure—he saw
The one subtending truth compared to which
All others dwindle: our human kind is passing away—
Being replaced—we're replacing ourselves; we
Are the first species that has consciously
Shifted its ecological niche;
We exempt ourselves from Nature's law.

DNA was unspooled in the year
I was born, and the test-tube births
Of cloned mammals emerged in a mere
Half century; it seems the Earth's
Future's now in the hands of a few
Techies on a caffeinated all-nighter who
Sift the gene-alphabet like Scrabble tiles

And our computer geeks are revealed, at last,
As those quick-handed, sidelined little mammals
In the dinosaurs' long shadows—those least-
Likely-to-succeed successors whose kingdom come
Was the globe itself (an image best written down,
Perhaps, beneath a streetlamp, late, in some
Star-riddled Midwestern town).

He wrote boy's books and intuitively
Recognized that the real
Realist isn't the one who details
Lowdown heartland factories and farms
As if they would last, but the one who affirms,
From the other end of the galaxy,
Ours is the age of perilous miracles.

We're learning to remake ourselves. We think
We see the danger; therein lies the danger.
The Earth moves. It hauls to the light the dark houses
Whose sleepers wake to a dawn wherein
They do not know their children, or their spouses,
And the mirror above the bathroom sink
Returns the fixed, confident gaze of a stranger.

THE ARACHNID'S TRIUMPH:
A ONE-ACT

In the stark theater in the round
   of a rubber plant leaf
a hunchback, backlit by a blood-red sun,
carts a body offstage, and though the brief,
   skeletal drama's nearly done

   its argument remains uncertain;
      even so, we must praise
the enterprise of a performer who,
without a wasted move, not only plays
   the lead but sews the final curtain.

EMIGRANT'S STORY

(Apulia, 1898)

They did not mean
To make fun of the departing sister who stood
In tears as *La Buona Fortuna* set sail,
Weeping into the noise
Of the whistles and the shouts, but the scene
Was so festive!—
                and they were boys,
Ages eight and six, and it soon became
A laughing, shoving sort of game

As they raced up the hill, in a mad flight
To see which one of them would
Be the very last to catch sight
Of the lucky sister, age ten,
Who stood in tears at the rail,
Whom neither would see again.

AN OLD STUMP

The sun rarely shines in history,
what with the dust and confusion.

THOREAU

The fine crack
that ranges through the rings
cuts a path through Time itself, and to track
its retrocessive wanderings
back from the barked rim

toward the heartwood core
is progressively to clear away
the brush of the years, bit by bit restore
the far and flourishing heyday
of that just-come spring

when, right here,
in a chill cell, buried pin-
prick promptings began to cohere—
warmed, firmed, and with a crust-fissuring
upthrust, found the sun.

SOME WAYS ALONG

The gold leaves

That hang so tough
As the wind heaves,
Seeing the storm through,

Will flutter down
At the merest puff
When, in a week or two,

Gold is brown.

64° NORTH

A frozen inland sea, and New Year's Day.
Two forms of water—a white
lacing of frost, then ice, steel gray.
The year's longest night

now stands a week behind us, the planet's great
axial shifting begun,
ultimately to culminate
in a midnight sun

and a breeze-whitecapped lake, blue as a true sea,
though on this New Year's Day
that firm eventuality
looks as far away

as the row of low white hills on the horizon
that lets the hiker know
miles of ice give way in time
to rock and snow.

A FURTHER FORAY

Our aircraft might have been a diver,
outfitted with a mask, fins, and an air tank,
   in neutral buoyancy between
the coral-reef sprawl of the cumulus bank
below us and the sun-clasped surface of
   the cirrus lid above.

But—with something missing: where are
   the creatures of the reef? The quick
crustaceans in their springy
   armor, loose eels, the jeweled schools
of fry? And what of those fleshed anemones
   whose threshing seems a winnowing
of the very light from out the sea?

Here we find the niches, all the rich
   recesses needed to sustain a thriving
tenantry; here's the risky yet
   irresistible promise of cover,
food, offspring—but toward
   what end? Where's the life of the reef?
Ah, there it is: dim in the distance,

   one glint of a scaled flank. . . . Look closer,
though, and it's only a fellow diver, making
   off in the other direction: a needle
in search of
      a haystack, a hive, a hum, seeking
the independent stir
      that must be here,
   flourishing somewhere.

A NOTE ABOUT THE AUTHOR

Brad Leithauser is the author of five previous collections of poetry, six novels,
a novel in verse, two collections of light verse, and a book of essays. Among
the many awards and honors he has received are a Guggenheim Fellowship, an
Ingram Merrill grant, and a MacArthur Fellowship. He served for a year as *Time*
magazine's theater critic. He is a professor in the Writing Seminars at Johns
Hopkins University. In 2005, Leithauser was inducted into the Order of the
Falcon by the president of Iceland for his writings about Nordic literature.

A NOTE ON THE TYPE

The text of this book was set in Bembo, a facsimile of a typeface cut by
Francesco Griffo for Aldus Manutius, the celebrated Venetian printer, in 1495.
The face was named for Pietro Cardinal Bembo, the author of the small treatise
entitled *De Aetna* in which it first appeared. Through the research of Stanley
Morison, it is now generally acknowledged that all oldstyle type designs up to
the time of William Caslon can be traced to the Bembo cut.
The present-day version of Bembo was introduced by the Monotype
Corporation of London in 1929. Sturdy, well-balanced, and finely proportioned,
Bembo is a face of rare beauty and great legibility in all of its sizes.

COMPOSED BY *North Market Street Graphics, Lancaster, Pennsylvania*

PRINTED AND BOUND BY *Thomson Shore, Dexter, Michigan*

DESIGNED BY *Iris Weinstein*